CHURCH NOW KINGDOM LATER

Randal D. Reese

Church Now Kingdom Later

Copyright © 2019 by Randal D. Reese

Published by Until That Day Ministries, Mansfield, Georgia

All rights reserved. No part of this book may be reproduced, stored in a retrieval system, or transmitted in any form by any means—electronic, mechanical, photocopy, recording, or other—without the prior written permission of the publisher.

Scripture references are from the King James Version of the Bible.

Cover and interior design: Katie Caron
Cover photos: Adobe Stock/stock.adobe.com

ISBN: 978-0-578-61220-1

Printed in the United States of America

I would like to dedicate this book to my Dad,
Robert W. Reese.
He has been a huge inspiration and encouragement,
not only in the writing of this book (critiquing the dissertation),
but also for the last twenty-nine years while pastoring
New Rocky Creek Baptist Church. I treasure his insight,
hindsight, and foresight. He has been blessed with a fruitful
ministry of teaching Sunday School and is currently,
handing down a lasting legacy!
I thank God for a Christian Dad!

"... the glory of children are their fathers."
Proverbs 17:6

Contents

Introduction 7

1. The King's Revelation of the Kingdom
   (Old Testament) 13

2. The King's Invitation to the Kingdom
   (Gospels and Acts) 23

3. The King's (Bridegroom) Evacuation of the Church Before
   the Kingdom (Epistles) 35

   Post-Tribulation (Chronological, Biblical, Practical) 43
   Pre-Wrath (Historical and Prophetical) 44
   Response to Pre-Wrath (Prophetical, Exegetical, Chron.) 45
   Pre-Tribulation (Chronological and Exegetical) 51
   Pre-Tribulation (Prophetical) 52
   Pre-Tribulation (Grammatical and Hermeneutical) 54
   Pre-Tribulation (Practical and Historical) 55

4. The King's Preservation of the Church Before the Kingdom
   (Revelation 2-3) 61

   The Kingdom in the Epistles of Paul 64
   The Kingdom in Peter, James, and John 78
   The Kingdom and Overcomers 81
   The Church and the Kingdom – Judgment Seat "bema" 88

5. The King's Inauguration of the Kingdom
   (Rev. 19-20, Ezek. 40-48) 99

   Millennium – 1000 years 103
   Millennium (Kingdom) Theological Views 104
   Exegetical Study of Revelation and Kingdom 110
   Millennium (Kingdom) Conditions on Earth 112
   The Church in the Kingdom 117
   Kingdom of Satan 119
   Kingdom of Nimrod 121
   Worship in the Kingdom (Ezekiel's – Messiah's Temple) 123
   Life in the Kingdom (Millennium) 130

6. The King's Destination of the Earthly and Eternal Kingdom
   (Rev. 21-22) 137

7. The King's (Bridegroom) Preparation for His Church Prior
   to the Kingdom (Rom. 6-8) 147

   Spirit-Filled Living Versus Kingdom Authority 149
   Fellowship for the Church Now Preparing for the Kingdom 151

Conclusion 155

Bibliography 159

About the Author 173

Introduction

Is the kingdom now? Or is it later? There are those who claim the church is now in the kingdom. Are there enough biblical evidences to justify that position? Conversely, there are those who teach the kingdom is yet to come in a futuristic event. Can both be correct? Does the Bible indicate which is true?

The purpose of this book is to attempt to clarify the correct view with the understanding that God's universal kingdom is in operation controlling the earth and the universe. This does not include the church functioning in the kingdom at the present time. Though not exhaustive on the subject, the goal is to present the information found in the different views and to compare them with the Scriptures. This research will examine both the Old and New Testament and explain how the church fits into God's purpose for His kingdom. The church's relation to the kingdom will be explored from a historical, exegetical, hermeneutical, grammatical, doctrinal, contextual, and practical perspective.

Influences from theological presuppositions, as well as cultural and political persuasions, seem to sway personal opinion. Dominion theology advocates the church is ushering in an end-time revival and ultimately Christ's return. What is Christian Dominionism?

> *Dominionism*, or *Christian Dominionism* is a term coined by social scientists and popularized by journalists to refer to a subset of American Christianity

that is conservative, politically active, and believes that Christians should, and eventually will, take control of the government. The term is sometimes used as a "catch-all" by bloggers to describe any politically active Christian, but not every conservative, politically minded Christian is a Dominionist. Christian Dominionists believe that God desires Christians to rise to power through civil systems so that His Word might then govern the nation. Dominion theology's beliefs are based on Genesis 1:28, which says, 'Be fruitful, and multiply, and replenish the earth, and subdue it: and have dominion over the fish of the sea, and over the fowl of the air, and over every living thing that moveth upon the earth.'[1]

This movement can be observed today, both in politics and in the church. However, this does not negate the Christian's responsibility to be "salt and light" in this culture.

Various denominations have utilized catch phrases such as "kingdom authority." Songwriters, past and present, have penned words that promote the idea that the kingdom is now expressed through the church.

> Majesty, worship his majesty
> Unto Jesus be all glory, power and praise
> Majesty, kingdom authority flow from his throne[2]

Popular praise song *Build Your Kingdom Here* also promotes kingdom now teaching.

> Build Your kingdom here …
> Set Your church on fire
> Win this nation back
> Change the atmosphere …

---

1 Got Questions Ministries, "What is Christian dominionism?", Got Questions, https://www.gotquestions.org/Christian-dominionism.html (accessed October 24, 2018).
2 Hayford, Jack. "Majesty", http://www.songlyrics.com/jack-hayford/majesty/lyrics (accessed November 1, 2018).

> Build Your kingdom here
> Holy Spirit come invade us now
> We are Your Church[3]

While these songs are effective and enjoyable, their message is kingdom now language. Christians of all walks have been indoctrinated by the message of the words–some unknowingly. Others have not taken the time to investigate to verify that the claims are true.

Churches have come together under the umbrella of ecclesiastical tolerance using this agenda. This has resulted in more participation in evangelism, which is commendable. While good things have taken place, there remains the danger of compromising doctrinal integrity just for the sake of ecclesiastical unity. Lastly, the intention of this research is not to question the sincerity or spirituality of the opposing views, but to present respectfully what seems to be the better view concerning the church's role in the kingdom.

How can the kingdom be here on earth at the present time without a king? A king naturally has a queen (Esther). Is the church the queen? There do not seem to be any references in the Bible to the church being the queen. Rather, the church is described as the bride of Christ (Eph. 5:25-27 [KJV]). Jesus is referred to as the Bridegroom (Rev. 19:7-8). At His second coming, He will be crowned "KING OF KINGS AND LORD OF LORDS" (Rev. 19:11-16). John wrote,

> And I saw heaven opened, and behold a white horse; and he that sat upon him *was* called Faithful and True, and in righteousness he doth judge and make war. His eyes *were* as a flame of fire, and on his head *were* many crowns; and he had a name written, that no man knew, but he himself. And he was clothed with a vesture dipped in blood: and his name is called The Word of God. And the armies *which were* in heaven followed him upon white horses, clothed in fine linen, white and clean. And out of his mouth goeth a sharp

---

3 Llewellyn, Chris, Gareth Gilkeson and Will Herron. Performed by Rend Collective. "Build Your Kingdom Here", https://www.lyrics.com/lyric/28958242/Build+Your+Kingdom+Here (accessed November 1, 2018).

> sword, that with it he should smite the nations: and he shall rule them with a rod of iron: and he treadeth the wine press of the fierceness and wrath of Almighty God. And he hath on *his* vesture and on his thigh a name written, "KING OF KINGS, AND LORD OF LORDS.

When the King returns, He will establish or set up His kingdom, but not until then.

Scripturally, Jesus is presently at the right hand of the Father. "Who *is* he that condemneth? *It is* Christ that died, yea rather, that is risen again, who is even at the right hand of God, who also maketh intercession for us" (Rom. 8:34).

> Hath in these last days spoken unto us by *his* Son, whom he hath appointed heir of all things, by whom also he made the worlds; Who being the brightness of *his* glory, and the express image of his person, and upholding all things by the word of his power, when he had by himself purged our sins, sat down on the right hand of the Majesty on high (Heb. 1:1-3).

Therefore, the conclusion is that the literal kingdom of Christ on the earth is not in operation at the present time. While it is true, the Holy Spirit was sent on the day of Pentecost, as Jesus promised, and as is recorded in Acts Chapter 2, the ultimate purpose of this event was to evangelize the world. Though Jesus made this promise, it did not fulfill the unconditional covenants God made with Israel. The fulfillment of these covenants will be complete only when Jesus sets up His kingdom on earth.

One obvious problem with the kingdom now concept (through the church) is the misunderstanding of the function of the church and the proper eschatological interpretation of Scripture. Another difficulty with the kingdom now authority (through the church), otherwise known as Dominion theology, is that it confuses the real intention for the literal kingdom. Is the church supposed to usher in the kingdom? While the kingdom now theology does create some confusion, it does not diminish the role of the church on earth before Christ's kingdom comes. This discussion prompts the following questions: (1) What role, from a biblical perspective, does the church play in the kingdom? (2) Why is it important to differentiate between the kingdom now (involving the church) and the kingdom later at the second coming of Christ? (3) Can one observe a kingdom now (church) functioning in the same manner as the Bible describes the kingdom to come in Revelation 20 (without Satan's interference)? (4) Are there two kingdoms, one for the church and one for Israel? (5) Was the church given the kingdom after Jesus departed or was the kingdom intended for the literal millennial reign of Christ (see Acts 1:5-7)? (6) Can one acknowledge God's universal kingdom without teaching the kingdom now through the church? (7) Is the kingdom meant to be a time when Paul said, "All of Israel will be saved" (Rom. 11:26)? (8) Can one see from the Bible that Israel (not the church) will be the fulfillment of God's promises when they turn to their Messiah and trust Him during this futuristic event called the millennial kingdom on earth (see Isa. 63:1-4; Zech. 3:9; Rev. 12:6; Matt. 24:16)? (9) Is there a lack of evidence for the church to be in the kingdom now? (10) Just because the church has been given Holy Spirit power, should one read into the Scriptures and assume the church is in the kingdom age (ruling and having control)? (11) Did God intend for the bride of Christ to have a kingdom now on earth or to be married to the bridegroom in heaven and then participate in the kingdom on earth later?

This study will examine the following: God's establishment of the kingdom, Jesus' offer of the kingdom, the Lord's plan for His church in the event called the rapture which happens before the kingdom, the inauguration of the kingdom, God's preservation of the church prior to the kingdom, the relationship between the church and the kingdom, and finally the eternal state of the church following the kingdom.

The discovery of His eternal kingdom in both the Old and the New Testament will be a focus of this study. Another purpose will be to examine God's intention for His church in relation to His kingdom and eternity future, while remaining true to His promises to Abraham and David, and their descendants.

Chapter One

The King's Revelation of the Kingdom (Old Testament)

Kingdom Disciples is a Bible study written by Dr. Tony Evans. This study was released and printed in 2018. Evans defines the goal of kingdom disciples. "To live transformed lives that transfer the values of the kingdom of God to the earth so that they replicate themselves in the lives of others."[1] According to Evans, this act will be God duplicating His authority and rule from heaven to earth through His disciples (the church). He further states, "The church would be the new mechanism through which God would express His kingdom rule in history until such a time He renewed it with His people Israel."[2]

Alva McClain, writing from a different perspective than Evans, mentions the following: "The error of identifying the Kingdom with the Church, followed by the logical attempt of certain ecclesiastical organizations to exercise during the present age a regal authority which belongs to the true Church in a future Kingdom, has been the source of untold evil and disaster."[3] McClain speaking on Matthew 16:18-19, writes that this authority given to the church is intended to be exercised in the kingdom of heaven. According to McClain, this is future.

---

1   Tony Evans, *Kingdom Disciples* (Nashville, TN: Lifeway, 2018), 16.
2   Ibid., 38.
3   Alva J. McClain, *The Greatness of the Kingdom* (Winona Lake, IN: BMH Pub., 1959), 329.

Writing concerning the kingdom and the church, Craig Blaising and Darrell Bock relate, "All who come to faith in Jesus are likewise blessed by the gift of the Spirit and join this kingdom community, which has come to be known as the church."[4] This view is derived from Progressive Dispensationalism. Based on the same teaching, Fred Klooster states,

> The presence of the kingdom is evident in the New Covenant, the church of Jesus Christ, and in every manifestation of kingdom life on the part of believers is … All believers are citizens of that kingdom. The realm of Christ's kingdom is present in Christian families, Christian schools, the church, and wherever life is lived in obedience to the king, wherever Christians 'seek first his kingdom and his righteousness' (Matt. 6:33).[5]

This view of the church in the kingdom is a compromise between the traditional teaching of Dispensationalism and Covenant Theology, which teaches that the church replaces Israel.

Stanley Toussaint, in a commentary on Matthew's gospel, wrote and listed three aspects concerning the kingdom.

> First, the earthly literal kingdom was offered to Israel in the person of Jesus, the Messiah, at His first coming. Second, the kingdom was postponed because Israel's rejected its Messiah. This postponed kingdom will be established at Christ's second coming. Third, Christ Jesus is now engaged in building His church, composed of those who in this age are heirs of the kingdom.[6]

This author concludes that Toussaint taught the kingdom is not here

---

4 Craig A. Blaising and Darrell L. Bock, *Progressive Dispensational* (Grand Rapids, MI: Baker Book House Co., 1993), 255.
5 John S. Feinberg, *Continuity and Discontinuity* (Wheaton, IL: Crossway Books, 1988), 159.
6 Stanley D. Toussaint, *Behold the King* (Grand Rapids, MI: Kregel Pub., 1980), 20.

on earth; rather it will be inaugurated during the millennial reign of Christ.

In his book, *Systematic Theology*, Wayne Grudem notes, "The kingdom manifests itself through the church, and thereby the future reign of God breaks into the present (it is already here, and not yet here fully)."[7] Clearly, the teaching of the kingdom experienced through the church is evident in Grudem's writings. In his discussion on the rapture, he notes that it is best to conclude that the church will go through the tribulation. This is opposite of the pre-tribulation rapture.[8]

Opposing Grudem, Charles Ryrie teaches the distinction between the kingdom and the church. In his book, *Dispensationalism*, he writes, "Because of the distinctions dispensationalists draw between the programs of God for the church and for the kingdom, it is often assumed that there is no relationship between the two."[9] He explains further. "In relation to the future millennial kingdom, dispensationalists have always taught that the church will share in the rule of that kingdom."[10] In his scholarly, but fair study on the subject, Ryrie teaches the importance of gaining all the facts before drawing conclusions. This is called inductive Bible study.

There is much misunderstanding and confusion concerning how and when the church relates to the kingdom (meaning God's millennial kingdom). For years, this writer was taught that God's kingdom is now and the church is building it. A closer and more thorough investigation of the Bible reveals a different interpretation. After researching and writing on this subject, starting in Genesis and continuing to Revelation, a student of the Bible should be able to see how God's kingdom plan fits in the past and unfolds in the future. Additionally, it is important to clarify the church's role during Christ's millennial kingdom.

In order to understand the concepts of the kingdom, kingdom must be defined. The Hebrew word is *malkuth* and is defined as "king

---

7   Wayne Grudem, *Systematic Theology* (Grand Rapids, MI: Inter-Varsity Press, 1994), 844.
8   Ibid, 1135.
9   Charles C. Ryrie, *Dispensationalism* (Chicago, IL: Moody Publishers, 2007), 157.
10   Ibid., 157.

dom, sovereignty, dominion, reign."[11] It is used ninety-one times in the Hebrew Bible. The word *mamlakaah* is used one hundred seventeen times in the Old Testament and is translated kingdom, sovereignty, dominion, and reign. The Greek word is *basileia*. It means "kingdom, sovereignty, royal power."[12] Webster defines kingdom as "A politically organized community or major territorial unit having a monarchical form of government headed by a king or queen."[13]

McClain writes, "The kingdom of God is, in a certain and important sense, the grand central theme of all Holy Scripture."[14] Vlach quotes McClain in describing the three essential elements in the kingdom concept. "(1) A Ruler with authority and power; (2) A Realm of subjects to be ruled; (3) A Rulership which involves carrying out the ruling."[15] In summary, a kingdom involves one being over in authority and power, a ruler. Secondly, a kingdom involves one being in authority and power over others or things being in subjection. Thirdly, a kingdom involves one being over by exercising power and authority. Vlach points out that these three elements are essential because there are teachers, for example George Ladd, who recognize the word kingdom to include authority and power but not territory or subjects.[16] This leads to a misunderstanding of the kingdom in its entirety.

Correct hermeneutics, or the proper interpretation of these words and concepts, results in the correct theological understanding of the kingdom in relation to the church.

Covenant theologians are known for their allegorical approach to the interpretation of Scripture. Consequently, from the covenant perspective, the church is the fulfillment of the covenants given to Israel. The dispensationalist draws a distinction between the two.

---

11   Blue Letter Bible, "H-4467 – mamlakah – Strong's Hebrew Lexicon (KJV)", https://www.blueletterbible.org//lang/lexicon/lexicon.cfm?Strongs=H4467&t=KJV (accessed October 24, 2018).
12   Ibid., "G-932 - basileia - Strong's Greek Lexicon (KJV)", https://www.blueletterbible.org//lang/lexicon/lexicon.cfm?Strongs=G932&t=KJV (accessed October 24, 2018).
13   *Merriam-Webster.com*, 2011. "kingdom." https://www.merriam-webster.com/dictionary/kingdom (accessed October 24, 2018).
14   McClain, 4-5.
15   Michael J. Vlach, *He Will Reign Forever* (Silverton, OR: Lampion Press, 2017), 28.
16   Ibid., 29.

Thus, from the literal interpretation, one sees the fulfillment of the Abrahamic, Davidic, Land, and New Covenant during the literal—not spiritual—period of the millennium on earth in Jerusalem (Rev. 20; Gen. 12-15; 2 Sam. 7:12-14; Jer. 31; Deut. 30). The Abrahamic, Davidic, Land, and New Covenant were all unconditional. However, as Dwight Pentecost points out, the blessings were conditional upon obedience. Speaking on the Abrahamic Covenant, Pentecost wrote:

> The eternal aspects of this covenant which guarantee Israel a permanent national existence, perpetual title to the land of promise, and the certainty of the material and spiritual blessing through Christ, and guarantee gentile nations a share in these blessings, determine the whole eschatological program of the word of God.[17]

To demonstrate that this covenant was unconditional, the Lord put Abraham to sleep and passed through the sacrifices, thus signifying it was unconditional (Gen. 15:7-21; Jer. 34:18). This covenant was established with Abraham and his physical seed, or descendants, forever. God told Abraham it was an everlasting covenant (Gen. 17:4, 6-7). God also reaffirmed His covenant with Jacob, who was Abraham's physical grandson (Gen. 28:13-17, 35:9-12, 48:34). Even Joseph, who was Abraham's great grandson, understood this covenant (Gen. 50:24-25).

The Abrahamic Covenant included personal promises, national promises, and universal promises. The personal promise was made by God to bless Abraham and make him a blessing to others (Gen. 12:2, 13:16, 15:4-5, 17:6). The national promise to Abraham concerned Israel, namely Jerusalem. His physical seed would become a great nation (Gen. 12:2), and his lineage would affect all the peoples of the world. Jesus made mention of this promise, which is to be fulfilled in the kingdom. This will be in the future (Matt. 25:31-46).

Renald Showers points out in *There Really is a Difference* that the Davidic covenant has three major components or promises (2

---

17   Dwight Pentecost, *Things to Come* (Grand Rapids, MI: Zondervan, 1958), 71.

Sam. 7:4-7, 12-16).[18] Based on 2 Samuel 7:16, God promised David, "Thine house shall be established forever before thee." Showers writes the term "thine house" is a reference to David's physical seed.[19] Even though David's seed committed sin, God declared He would not abolish His covenant with David in Jerusalem (2 Chron. 21:7; Psa. 89:3-4, 36). Secondly, God foretold of David's "Kingdom" that would not pass away, although for a season it would not be functioning (2 Sam. 7:16). Thirdly, God declared his "throne would be established forever." Gabriel the angel confirmed this promise at the birth of Jesus, who was David's descendant (Luke 1:32-33).

The covenant theologian sees these promises as fulfilled by the church instead of a literal fulfillment in the millennium. Covenant theology is based on three major covenants—the covenant of works, grace, and redemption.[20] Their conclusion is based on the main promise, which is found in Genesis 17:7, where Moses wrote, "I will … be a God unto thee, and to thy seed after thee."

The difference in the Amillennialists' (kingdom now) view and the Premillennialists' (kingdom after second coming of Christ) view is the timing. Showers writes, "Amillennialists believe that Christ fulfills these promises now (during this age before His Second Coming) in His present rule over the Church or human hearts as He sits at the right hand on the throne of God in heaven."[21] He concludes that this teaches a spiritual kingdom only rather than a literal and political kingdom on earth. He makes a valid point when he writes, "Christ will rule, not just over the Church or individual human hearts yielded to Him, but over the entire earth (Ps. 72:8; Zech. 9:10; Dan. 2:35, 44-45)."[22] There are differing views as to when the Davidic Covenant will be fulfilled. Dispensationalists teach that it will be fulfilled when Jesus comes to rule and reign for a thousand years (Rev. 20:1-10).

Covenant theology considers both the Old and the New Testament Covenants to be the same (Matt. 26). Each dispensation or covenant is just another stage of progressive revelation. Therefore, there

---

18   Renald Showers, *There Really is a Difference* (Bellmawr, NR: The Friends of Israel Ministry Inc., 1990), 85.
19   Ibid., 86.
20   Ibid., 8-9.
21   Ibid., 88-89.
22   Ibid., 93.

is not the distinction between Israel and the Church with covenant theology, as there is with dispensationalism. Dispensationalists see all the covenants, the Abrahamic, Davidic, Land, and New, as completely being fulfilled in a literal way with Israel during the future second coming of Christ and in the millennium.[23]

Instead of a literal, grammatical, and historical interpretation (2 Pet. 1:19-21; 2 Tim. 3:16), the covenant theologian uses an allegorical approach to the Bible.[24] Progressive dispensationalists also blur the hermeneutical lines of interpretation when they advocate the already but not yet method concerning the fulfillment of the Davidic Covenant.[25] Ryrie writes, "In American evangelicalism the writings of George E. Ladd widely promoted views of the kingdom are now embraced by progressive dispensationalism."[26] The conclusion is that the lines of literal interpretation have shifted.

When it comes to the term kingdom, Charles Ryrie, a dispensationalist, recognized various types of kingdoms mentioned in the Bible. There appears to be a universal kingdom where God rules the world (1 Chron. 29:11; Psa.145:13). Furthermore, there is the Davidic (Messianic) kingdom which Jesus will rule over on the earth. The progressive dispensationalist teaches that Jesus is already ruling on the throne of David but not fully—the already but not yet concept.[27] In addition, there is a mystery kingdom mentioned in the parables which technically speaking, will be fulfilled in the millennium (Matt. 13). Paul referred to the kingdom of God's dear Son (Col. 1:13). Interpreting this passage, Michael Vlach writes that scholars such as Robert Saucy and David Farnell concur that although the term kingdom is in the aorist tense and has present realities, it favors an eschatological meaning for the kingdom.[28] Bible teachers and Christians must be able to study the passages of Scripture that mention the church and the kingdom using the proper interpretation.

As one can see, there are mixed views on the meaning of the phrase "the kingdom of God." The best view (dispensationalism) stands

---

23   Ryrie, *Dispensationalism*, 172.
24   Pentecost, *Things to Come* (Grand Rapids, MI: Zondervan, 1958), 4-8.
25   Ryrie, *Dispensationalism*, 189-209.
26   Ibid., 195.
27   Ibid., 101-102.
28   Vlach, 448-449.

above the rest because of its commitment to the literal, grammatical, historical hermeneutics of the bible; the distinction between Israel and the Church; and its ultimate goal of glorifying God.[29] Starting and finishing with the correct interpretation is non-negotiable.

Charles Feinberg verifies the kingdom can be traced back to the Old Testament. He writes, "The unwavering contention is that it is to be clearly seen in both the Old and New."[30] McClain concurs and explains, "The field of the Old Testament prophecy is not only the largest but also in certain respects the most important area in the entire investigation of the future Mediatorial Kingdom of God."[31] According to McClain, two kingdoms are revealed in the Bible. One is the "mediatorial" and the other is the "universal."[32] Speaking on the importance of the prophetic utterances of the Old Testament prophets, McClain writes if one is going to understand what Jesus said about the kingdom, they must first consider what the Old Testament prophets have said about it; furthermore, if one is going to expound the book of Revelation, they must begin with the book of Daniel.[33]

Vlach asks the question. How does the Old Testament relate to the New and how does the New use the Old?[34] Taking it a step further, he says, "The New does not reinterpret the Old or transcend the Old expectations."[35] In summary, he explains, "The kingdom promised in the Old Testament is the kingdom the New Testament revealed."[36] How does one confuse the Old with the New? Interpreting the passage in Isaiah 2:2-4, Vlach notes that John Calvin made this mistake. According to Calvin, this passage was "concerning the restoration of the church."[37] Rather, this passage in Isaiah Chapter Two is in reference to the kingdom period when the nation of Israel will inherit her land. During this millennial reign of Christ in His kingdom, there will be perfect peace and harmony as described in Isaiah.

---

29   Ryrie, *Dispensationalism*, 46-48.
30   Charles L. Feinberg, *Millennialism* (Winona Lake, IN: BMH Pub., 1985), 107.
31   McClain, 135.
32   Ibid., 21.
33   Ibid., 6.
34   Vlach, 32.
35   Ibid., 38.
36   Ibid., 41.
37   John Calvin, *Commentary on Isaiah-Volume 1*, Christian Classics Ethereal Library (Grand Rapids, MI: n.d.), 66, quoted in Vlach, 151.

Questions for Review and Discussion

1. What does the word "Kingdom" mean?
2. Why do you think the phrase "Kingdom of God" has been suggested as the grand central theme of all of Scripture?
3. Is there a distinct difference in the "Universal Kingdom" of God in which we live presently and the literal, physical "Kingdom of God" where Jesus (as King) sits on His throne on earth to rule and reign?
4. Describe the main difference in an amillennialist and a premillennialist?
5. Compare the allegorical approach (Covenant) to interpreting Scripture with the literal, grammatical, historical approach (dispensational). How do the two compare or contrast when it comes to Israel and the church?
6. Name the four major covenants listed in the Old Testament. Have these been fulfilled or will they be fulfilled in the future-during the kingdom?
7. How did God demonstrate with Abraham that His covenant was unconditional?
8. Discuss the different parts of the Abrahamic and Davidic Covenant and be able to find their location in the Bible.
9. How does the kingdom of the Old Testament relate to the kingdom of the New Testament?

Chapter Two

The King's Invitation to the Kingdom (Gospels and Acts)

Did Jesus set up His kingdom on earth and leave it to the church? Is the church presently in the kingdom? Was the nation of Israel offered the kingdom? Did they reject the kingdom? What does that mean? Has the kingdom been postponed? Will it be offered again?

When the time came for Jesus to arrive on earth from eternity past (John 1:1-5; Col. 1:16-17), establishing the kingdom was on His agenda. His kingdom was authenticated by His numerous miracles which included raising the dead (John 11; Luke 7; Mark 5), casting out demons (Mark 5:1-21), and healing disease (John 5:1-9, 9:1-7; Mark 5:22-34). Furthermore, the proclamation of the angels to Zechariah, Mary, and the shepherds (Luke 1:11-17, 26-35; 2:8-15; Matt 2:1-6), was intended to introduce His kingdom.

When Jesus came to earth, He came offering the kingdom of God to the Jews. Matthew wrote,

> From that time Jesus began to preach, and to say, Repent: for the kingdom of heaven is at hand… These twelve Jesus sent forth, and commanded them, saying, Go not into the way of the Gentiles, and into *any* city of the Samaritans enter ye not: But go rather to the lost sheep of the house of Israel. And as ye go, preach,

saying, The kingdom of heaven is at hand (Matt. 4:17; 10:5-7).

Clearly, the focus was on Israel. Toussaint explains the threefold elements of the kingdom program.

> First, the literal earthly kingdom was offered to Israel in the person of Jesus, the Messiah, at His first coming. Second, the kingdom was postponed because Israel rejected its Messiah. This postponed kingdom will be established at Christ's second coming. Third, Christ Jesus is now engaged in building His church, composed of those who in this age are heirs of the kingdom.[1]

In summary, Toussaint recognizes the church is now in God's program to join with Israel later during Christ's kingdom. Joseph Dillow concurs with this conclusion and writes, "The kingdom has been postponed and delayed for several thousand years precisely for this purpose, to raise up a body of rulers who will sustain it with dignity, purity, compassion, and selflessness worthy of the Messiah Jesus."[2]

In the same vein, Vlach explains Jesus' invitation to Israel. "Early on, Jesus' proclamation was limited to Israel. This must mean more than a courtesy call to the O.T. people of God as if Israel gets the first shot at the kingdom before everyone else."[3] Refuting the idea that this was only a personal invitation to salvation, Vlach writes, "Why proclaim it only to Israel? There must be a national element—and there is."[4] It becomes obvious that Jesus had His focus on fulfilling His promises to His people, the Jews, and yet He knew the fulfillment would be delayed.

Biblical evidence reveals the kingdom was postponed. Jesus said, "Therefore say I unto you, The kingdom of God shall be taken from you, and given to a nation bringing forth the fruits thereof" (Matt.

---

[1] Toussaint, 20.
[2] Joseph Dillow, *The Reign of the Servant Kings* (Hayesville, NC: Schoettle Pub., 1992), 595.
[3] Vlach, 276.
[4] Ibid., 277.

21:43). Luke wrote concerning the kingdom being rejected and thus delayed, as recorded in Luke 19:11. "And as they heard these things, he added and spake a parable, because he was nigh to Jerusalem, and because they thought that the kingdom of God should immediately appear." From these texts, it seems evident to conclude that Jesus' kingdom on earth had been postponed.

Toussaint writes, "The kingdom is postponed and the promises are yet to be fulfilled. The promises to Israel are not cancelled because it failed to accept its King at His first coming (Matt. 19:28, 20:20-23, 23:39, 24:29-31, 25:31-46)."[5] Ryrie clarifies some misunderstanding concerning salvation for the Jews. He notes, "Dispensationalists do not say that the postponed kingdom concept makes the Cross theoretically unnecessary or that it detracts from the glory of the church."[6] He concurs with L.S. Chafer by stating, "There is no kingdom for Israel apart from the suffering Savior, as well as the reigning King."[7] The prophet Zechariah foretold that event. Israel shall look upon the one they pierced and mourn (Zech. 12:10) and be saved in a day (Zech. 3:9). Paul spoke of that time (Rom. 11:25-26). Jesus will become king of all the earth (Zech. 14:9). Arguing in favor of those who teach the postponement, Feinberg states,

> The millenarians do not maintain that the only purpose of God's coming was to set up a kingdom. He came to offer the kingdom to Israel, to reveal the Father, to put away sins, to destroy the works of Satan, to leave His followers an example, to provide a foundation for the church, and to prepare for the second advent—all to glorify God.[8]

Feinberg explains God's purpose for the kingdom.

Debating on the side of a present spiritual kingdom (already, but not yet), Blaising writes, "The kingdom which Jesus proclaimed was as much a spiritual as a physical kingdom."[9] He goes a step further

---

5   Toussaint, 19.
6   Charles Ryrie, *Basic Theology* (U.S.A.: Victor Books, 1988), 175.
7   Ibid., 176.
8   Charles L. Feinberg, *Millennialism*, 256.
9   Craig A. Blaising and Darrell L. Bock, *Progressive Dispensational*, 242.

in saying,

> We want to note Jesus' teaching on the mysteries of the kingdom which appear to give new revelation about the kingdom beyond that which we have seen so far. Included in the new revelation was the prediction of a form or stage of the kingdom's presence prior to its full and apocalyptic establishment.[10]

The "new revelation" seems to be the departure of the dispensationalist perspective on the future kingdom instead of the present kingdom, which is taught by progressive dispensationalists. This "new revelation" interprets the mystery parables as having present day implication. Blaising explains, "While it is not altogether clear in the parables that this newly revealed presence of the kingdom will follow the cross, it is clear that it is a stage which precedes the apocalyptic coming of the kingdom."[11] His interpretation leads to the teaching of the already kingdom concept.

In Matthew 19:28, Jesus reveals what will take place when He sits on His throne futuristically. He is discussing what rewards Peter will have for following him. Jesus says, "Verily I say unto you, that ye which have followed me, in the regeneration when the Son of Man shall sit in the throne of his glory, ye also shall sit upon twelve thrones, judging the twelve tribes of Israel." The word "regeneration"–*palingenesia* is only used two times in the New Testament (Titus 3:5-6; Matt. 19:28) and here means recreation and renewal.[12] According to Toussaint, based on Old Testament prophecy, any Israelite would have recognized that the Messiah would create a new heaven and earth (Isa. 65:17, 66:22).[13] Toussaint writes, "The Lord thus confirms the promise He had already given to Peter (Matthew 16:19) and enlarges it to include all of the apostles."[14]

---

10   Blaising and Bock, *Progressive Dispensational*, 251.
11   Ibid.
12   Blue Letter Bible, "G-3824 – palingenesia – Strong's Greek Lexicon (KJV)", https://www.blueletterbible.org//lang/lexicon/lexicon.cfm?Strongs=G3824&t=KJV (accessed November 13, 2018).
13   Toussaint, 228.
14   Ibid., 229.

However, Bloomberg commenting on Matthew 19:28, writes that Israel and the twelve disciples represent all humanity. He clarifies his position, "So we cannot conclude that the apostles necessarily receive any privilege they do not share with all believers. But the comparison of the twelve with the twelve tribes of Israel again highlights the theme of the church replacing Israel as the focus of God's saving activity in the new age."[15] Vlach argues against this idea and lists David Hill and Robert Mounce, who concur that the twelve tribes are the new Israel or the church.[16] McClain admits that Israel holds the main place in this discussion but Gentile nations will have a place in the kingdom.[17] He references Matthew 8:11, 10:5-6, and 12:17-21. These interpretational differences lead to different conclusions concerning the kingdom and the church. However, with proper hermeneutics, one should differentiate between Israel and the church in the kingdom.

Another issue of confusion is found in the interpretation of Luke 17:21. Speaking to the Pharisees concerning when the kingdom should come, Jesus says, "Behold, the kingdom of God is within you." What did He mean? There are those who claim this verse is a proof text that the kingdom is present. Is it? Commenting on Luke 17:21, Pentecost says, "The Lord was not asserting that His kingdom was to be a spiritual kingdom in the hearts of men. Such is contrary to the entire tenor of the Word of God."[18] He explains the kingdom of God was already at hand in Jesus, the king. Toussaint concurs, "While some say it means *within*, others say it is to be translated *among*. Of the two, *among* is far the better."[19]

Writing from the perspective of the present kingdom, Walter Kaiser states, "That kingdom is also present, in some sense, as well as yet future."[20] He lists some evidences of the kingdom's current presence (Col. 1:13; Heb. 12:28; Rev. 1:9; Matt. 13:18-19, 23; 12:28). According to Kaiser, the kingdom has both spiritual and material aspects, and

---

15   Craig L. Blomberg, *The New American Commentary, Matthew* (Nashville, TN: Broadman Press, 1992), 301.
16   Vlach, 345.
17   McClain, 295.
18   Pentecost, *Things to Come*, 452.
19   Toussaint, 163.
20   John S. Feinberg, *Continuity and Discontinuity* (Wheaton, IL: Crossway Books, 1988), 304.

soteriological and eschatological concepts. Craig Blomberg comments on the passage in Matthew 21:43, where Jesus speaks of the kingdom taken from Israel. Blomberg writes, "Jesus is not so much foreshadowing the shift of God's activity from Jewish to Gentile realms as anticipating the replacement of Israel by the church, which will unite both Jew and Gentile."[21] However according to the correct interpretation, Israel does not replace the church (replacement theology). Both the church and Israel will have their place in the kingdom to come.

If Jesus had intended for the church to fulfill His promises of a coming kingdom or existing kingdom as some teach, why would He not have told the disciples? Instead, He tells them it is not for them to know the time. The time would be left up to the Father. In the book of Acts, Luke the historian, revealed an important statement from Jesus to the disciples concerning the kingdom. "When they therefore were come together, they asked of him, saying, Lord, wilt thou at this time restore again the kingdom to Israel? And he said unto them, It is not for you to know the times or the seasons, which the Father hath put in his own power" (Acts 1:6-7). However, some authors interpret this passage from the perspective that the church would be called out while the kingdom had been delayed. J. Vernon McGee comments, "He let them know, at this particular time, that the kingdom would not be established. Rather, He would call out a people to His name, the church."[22] This view is not consistent with replacement theology.

Furthermore, several observations can be drawn from the Acts 1:6 text. The apostles were expecting the kingdom to be restored. The word "restore" (Greek-*apokathistemi*) means to restore again or to its former state.[23] McClain comments on the word "restore." "The tense of the verb is *futuristic* present, indicating an expectation as yet unrealized."[24] Both McClain and Vlach concur the focus of the apostles was on "when" the kingdom would come instead of "what" it

---

21   Blomberg, 325.
22   Vernon J. McGee, *Thru the Bible, Vol. 3* (Nashville, TN: Thomas Nelson, 1982), 511.
23   Blue Letter Bible, "G-600 – apokathistemi – Strong's Greek Lexicon (KJV)", https://www.blueletterbible.org//lang/lexicon/lexicon.cfm?Strongs=G600&t=KJV (accessed November 13, 2018).
24   McClain, 393.

would be. Finally, "The apostles did not view the kingdom as being in operation or inaugurated at this point."[25] That leads one to conclude that if the kingdom was established at Pentecost, the disciples would have noted it.

John Polhill interprets this passage (Acts 1:6-8) with several conclusions. "Jesus rejected speculation about the times altogether and in v.8 replaced this with the relevant subject – the Christian task in the interim period before the kingdom's coming."[26] He writes, "The disciples were to be the true "restored" Israel, fulfilling its mission to be a 'light for the Gentiles' so that God's salvation might reach 'to the ends of the earth' (Isa. 49:6)."[27] According to Polhill, the restoration of the kingdom involves a worldwide movement turned into a mission.

In summary, the kingdom was offered to Israel. The context of Acts 1:6 was written before the establishment of the church (Acts 2). The kingdom statements were directed to Israel, not the church. Israel had rejected their king and consequently, their kingdom. Therefore, it has been postponed until the king returns. In support, McClain emphasizes the importance of the absence of any mention of Jesus concerning the transfer of the kingdom to the church or the throne of David from the earth to heaven.[28]

Blaising argues in favor of the kingdom being present already through the church, but not fully. His argument is weak. Blaising builds his case on Jesus being identified with the Davidic Covenant. He writes, "It teaches that certain blessings of the Davidic covenant have already been granted to Jesus, while other blessings await His return."[29] His proof texts are found in Revelation 3:7; 5:5; 3:12; and 22:16, where Jesus is called the "root of David" and has the "key of David" and "the offspring of David." This view falls short due to Blaising's inability to reconcile the political fulfillment of Christ on earth and yet, He is at the right hand of the Father. A partial activity on earth through the church while Jesus is in heaven requires an interpretational stretch to accomplish. It seems best to stick with the

---

25 Vlach, 403.
26 John Polhill, *The New American Commentary*, vol. 26 (Nashville, TN: Broadman Press, 1982), 84-85.
27 Ibid., 85.
28 McClain, 394.
29 Craig A. Blaising and Darrell L. Bock, *Progressive Dispensational*, 181.

literal interpretation that is consistent with the whole Bible.

Vlach disputes the idea that the kingdom is already on earth through the church. He disagrees with the down payment theory that the Davidic Covenant is fulfilled by the church at the present time. Commenting on Acts 2:22-36, he asks the question, "Does Jesus' resurrection and ascension mean that He is currently reigning from David's throne in an already/not yet reign?"[30] Vlach answers by saying, "We do not think so. The preferred view is that the resurrection and ascension of Jesus means that Jesus currently shares all authority and power with the Father at the right hand, but the Davidic/Messianic reign awaits Jesus' second coming to earth."[31]

Another important passage in the book of Acts is 3:19-21. This event comes after the ascension of Jesus and the outpouring of the Holy Spirit on the early believers. Consequently, the church was established. This fulfilled the promise of Jesus (Luke 24:46-49). It was during the Feast of Pentecost when many Jews were present. After the healing of a crippled man, Peter addresses the "Men of Israel" (Acts 3:12). These men were the Jewish leaders who participated in putting Jesus to death (Acts 4:1). All of this had national implications.

Peter's message is directed to the Jews who acted in "ignorance" (Acts 3:17). The purpose is an attempt to give the Jews another chance. Polhill explains that Jesus mentions that they were in "ignorance" (Luke 23:34) and therefore, could be forgiven.[32] Some Jews considered "intentional" sins unforgiveable.

Peter declares, "Repent ye therefore, and be converted that your sins may be blotted out, when the times of refreshing shall come from the presence of the Lord" (Acts 3:19). According to Polhill, the word "repent" (*metanoeo*) and "turn to God" (*epistrepho*) was directed toward "the Jerusalem Jews who were to have a complete change of mind from their rejection of Christ and turning or returning to God."[33] According to Vlach, the phrase "times of refreshing" only occurs here in the New Testament and involves "rest and refreshment." It refers

---

30 Sam Storms, *Kingdom Come: The Amillenial Alternative* (Ross-sire, Scotland: Mentor, 2013), 301, quoted in Michael J. Vlach, *He Will Reign Forever* (Silverton OR: Lampion Press, 2017), 401.
31 Vlach, 411.
32 Polhill, 133.
33 Ibid., 134.

to an eschatological refreshment from God.[34] He explains that after Israel repents "he shall send Jesus Christ" (Acts 3:20). "This is a specific reference to the second coming of Jesus."[35] Furthermore, he declares God will do this not only for Israel, but for the whole earth and all nations (Rom. 9:4).[36]

Author McClain connects the word "restitution" to the two verses in Acts 1:6 and 3:19-21. According to McClain, Peter is referring to the kingdom spoken of in the Old Testament to be fulfilled at the second coming of Christ. He describes Acts 3:19-21, "We have something better than a term: actually, a definition of the kingdom."[37]

Other writers see it differently. Concurring with F.F. Bruce on the passage in Acts 3:19-21, and contrary to McClain and Vlach, Bruce Waltke writes, "No clear passage teaches the restoration of national Israel, its reverse side is imprinted with the hard fact that national Israel and its laws have been permanently replaced by the church and the New Covenant."[38] He explains according to Mark 12:1-9, Jesus announces the Jewish nation has been disqualified. He goes on to say, "That place has been taken by the Christian community which fulfills God's purpose for Israel."[39] Here again is a clear violation of the proper method of interpretation, which leads to erroneous conclusions.

Debating against the progressive dispensationalist view (kingdom already, but not yet), Ryrie points out some interpretational discrepancies. He tackles two phrases, "times of refreshing" and "restoration of all things" (Acts 3:19-21). According to progressive dispensationalists, the phrase "times of refreshing" refers to the present time (already) but the "restoration" refers to the future (not yet). However, Ryrie suggests that if that was the case, first of all those listening to Peter would not have understood him; in addition, there is a grammatical problem with that interpretation (already-kingdom now, but not yet-future kingdom theology). Ryrie points out the Greek word "*hopos*" in verse twenty connects a purpose. Two parts are included, "times of refreshing" and the coming of Christ. The first part "times

---
34   Vlach, 414.
35   Ibid., 415.
36   Ibid., 418.
37   McClain, 406.
38   John S. Feinberg, *Continuity and Discontinuity*, 274.
39   Ibid., 275.

of refreshing" are interpreted by the progressives as to the present time (already-now) and the latter as to the return of Christ. There is a problem. Ryrie explains,

> The construction links the two events: the times of refreshing (the millennial, Davidic kingdom) will come when Christ returns and not before. The two clauses (with two subjunctive verbs) that follow *hopos* cannot be separated, as progressives do, in order to support their already (present Davidic kingdom, the "times of refreshing") and not yet (future Davidic kingdom, "restoration of all things") concept.[40]

Admittedly, a wrong exegetical turn can lead to getting lost in understanding eschatology.

Tracing progressive dispensationalism teaching (kingdom already-but not yet), Ryrie listed prominent scholars back to 1926, such as C.H. Dodd. Dodd, along with George Ladd, Anthony Hoekema (an amillennialist), and R.C. Sproul all taught the concepts of the "already" Christ's present reign in partial fulfillment of the Davidic Covenant and the "not yet" in His millennial reign.[41] In conclusion, exegetical error paves the way for doctrinal danger.

Luke records the last words of Paul while in Rome. His message was on the kingdom of God. "And when they had appointed him a day, there came many to him into his lodging; to whom he expounded and testified the kingdom of God. Persuading them concerning Jesus, both out of the law of Moses, and out of the prophets, from morning till evening" (Acts 28:23). Who were those listening to Paul? Polhill writes, "Paul's second meeting with the Roman Jews involved considerably larger numbers (Acts 28:23). In Rome, however, there were no Gentile contingent: the audiences were solely Jews."[42] The Jewish crowd is significant. Paul's message would have been applicable to them especially after expounding on the Old Testament and then integrating the concepts of the New, namely the kingdom of God to

---

40 Ryrie, *Dispensationalism*, 199-200.
41 Ibid., 197.
42 Polhill, 541.

come. Furthermore, Jesus had explained that the time of the restoration of the kingdom for the Jews was in the Father's control (Acts 1:6; 3:17-21). McClain notes, "The main subject of discussion was the "kingdom of God" and the relation of "Jesus" to that kingdom."[43] While some believed, some did not believe. Israel was still blinded in unbelief.

Paul's focus was on the kingdom of God. In his last days, that was his message (Acts 19:8; 20:25; 26:7-8; 28:23). Vlach writes, "There is no indication here that Paul is telling these Jews about an alleged 'new Israel'. He is discussing the hope of national Israel, a hope rooted strongly in the O.T."[44]

However, what is known about the kingdom can be found in Luke's gospel. He will sit on His throne forever and His kingdom will not end. Gabriel explains, "He shall be called great, and shall be called the Son of the Highest: and the Lord God shall give unto him the throne of his father David: And he shall reign over the house of Jacob forever; and of his kingdom there shall be no end" (Luke 1:32-33).

Questions for Review and Discussion

1. How did Jesus authenticate His coming kingdom?
2. Technically speaking, to whom did Jesus offer the kingdom?
3. List the verses in the gospels where this is recorded.
4. Has the implementation of the kingdom of God been temporarily postponed but not cancelled?
5. Explain Luke 17:21. Please notice who Jesus is talking to at the time about the kingdom of God being within them.
6. Discuss the passage in Acts 1:6-7, where the disciples (Jews) ask Jesus about when the kingdom of God would come. Please notice this is chronologically before the establishment of the church (Acts 2), but the church would not fulfill the literal, physical completion of the kingdom of God (the kingdom was prom-

---

43   McClain, 422.
44   Vlach, 429.

ised to the Jewish people-see the last chapter and the references in the Old Testament).
7. Discuss the passages in Acts 3:19-21 and 28:23, in regards to the kingdom of God.

Chapter Three

The King's (Bridegroom) Evacuation of the Church Before the Kingdom (Epistles)

Is the church now in the kingdom? Does the King need to come first? Does the Bible teach the church should be looking for the Bridegroom before the King? Do the words church and Israel mean the same thing? How does one conclude the church is presently in the kingdom?

Defining terms is critical. Grudem writes, "The Septuagint translates the word for 'gather' (Hebrew, *qahal*) with the Greek term *ekklesiazo*, 'to summon an assembly,' the verb that is cognate to the New Testament noun *ekklesia*, 'church.'"[1] Grudem explains, "It is not surprising, then, that the New Testament authors can speak of the Old Testament people of Israel as a 'church' (*ekklesia*)."[2] If one defines the two words in the O.T. and N.T. the same, it stands to reason they are the same, thus integrating Israel and the church. This logic is where theologians and scholars depart from the literal, historical interpretation of Scripture. This leads to various views concerning the church including the rapture and the timing of the kingdom.

Describing the difference in the kingdom of God and the church,

---

1   Grudem, 854.
2   Ibid.

Grudem quotes George Ladd's approach to the subject. "The church is the community of the kingdom but never the kingdom itself."[3] According to Ladd, there are five specific aspects of the relationship between the kingdom and the church:

> (1) The church is not the kingdom (for Jesus and the early Christians preached that the kingdom of God was near, not that the church was near, and preached the good news of the kingdom, not the good news of the church: Acts 8:12, 19:8, 20:25, 28:23, 31). (2) The kingdom creates the church (for as people enter into God's kingdom they become joined to the human fellowship of the church). (3) The church witnesses to the kingdom (for Jesus said, 'this gospel of the kingdom will be preached throughout the whole world,' Matt. 24:14). (4) The church is the instrument of the kingdom (for the Holy Spirit, manifesting the power of the kingdom, works through the disciples to heal the sick and cast out demons, as he did in the ministry of Jesus: Matt. 10:8; Luke 10:17). (5) The church is the custodian of the kingdom (for the church has been given the keys of the kingdom of heaven: Matt. 16:19).[4]

Those who integrate the church and the kingdom into one develop a system that becomes the criterion for interpreting all other Scripture regardless of its literal meaning. This leads to the embracing of a post-tribulation view of the rapture or an amillennial view of the kingdom.

If the church is Israel and presently in the kingdom as Grudem and Ladd suggest, then what event does Paul articulate will happen in the future? How is the church to prepare for the rapture? Are there evidences that point to the correct timing of this event?

In reading the letters written by both Paul and John, one can easily conclude there will be an event when the church is taken away. This

---

3   Grudem, 863.
4   George Eldon Ladd, *A Theology of the New Testament*, 2nd Ed., (Grand Rapids, MI: Eerdmans, 1993), 111-119, quoted in Wayne Grudem, *Systematic Theology* (Grand Rapids, MI: Inter-Varsity Press, 1994), 863-864.

event is referred to as the "rapture." Though the literal word rapture is not mentioned, it is described by the phrase, "*caught up.*"

> For the Lord himself shall descend from heaven with a shout, with the voice of the archangel, and with the trump of God: and the dead in Christ shall rise first: Then we which are alive and remain shall be caught up together with them in the clouds, to meet the Lord in the air: and so shall we ever be with the Lord. Wherefore comfort one another with these words (1 Thess. 4:16-18).

Alan Hultberg explains the meaning of the phrase "caught up." "The term comes from the Latin verb *rapio* (I seize, I [violently] carry off), which is the Vulgate's equivalent of the root Greek verb *harpazo* (I seize, I snatch away)."[5] There is a continuous debate as to the timing of this event.

There are four prominent views concerning the timing of the rapture. Each view is arguably the best. The first rapture (view) to consider is the pre-wrath view. This teaches that the church will go through the first half of the tribulation and then be raptured in the last half of the tribulation. The second view is the mid-tribulation view, which teaches the church will go through the first half of the tribulation. The third view is the post-tribulation view. This teaches that the church will go through the entire tribulation period of seven years, only to be raptured at the end of the tribulation. Finally, the fourth view is the pre-tribulation view. It demonstrates the church will be "caught up" before the seven years of tribulation. Which view of the rapture is correct? All four cannot be right.

What problems are associated with the different views? How can one reconcile the major differences? Why believe in the pre-tribulation teaching? Reasons to support the pre-tribulation teaching are as follows:

1. It stays true and consistent to the literal, historical, and grammatical method of interpretation. This method of interpre-

---

5   Craig A. Blaising and Douglas J. Moo, *Three Views on the Rapture*, ed. Alan Hultberg and Stanley N. Gundry (Grand Rapids, MI: Zondervan, 2010), 11.

tation recognizes apocalyptic literature and when applicable, relies upon a proper guideline to interpret such literature. Apocalyptic literature is symbolic language used to convey truth. Symbolic language can be interpreted by other Scripture (see example, Rev. 4:1-3).

2. It works out the confusion concerning the tribulation and the judgments, specifically the timing of God's wrath. It places God's wrath at the beginning of the tribulation (Rev. 5-6), rather than three-and-a-half years (mid-trib view) or five-and-a-half years into the tribulation (pre-wrath view).

3. It explains the phrase "the day of the Lord" and unifies the way it is used in both the Old and New Testament. "The day of the Lord" is a time of God's judgment and gloom during the tribulation, yet it is a time of His blessing during the millennial. It includes catastrophic signs that will affect heavenly bodies such as the sun, moon, and earth. These things cannot be explained properly by allegorical hermeneutics (opposite of literal). Furthermore, it connects the key passages of Daniel 2, 7, 8, 9, and 12, and Joel 2, etc., with the Olivet discourse of Matthew 24, in a unified and timely manner (ex. the "Abomination of Desolation"—Dan. 9:26-27, and Matt. 24:15). It does so both historically and futuristically by staying true to the text (proper hermeneutics).

4. It allows time for a remnant (saved tribulation saints) to prepare to enter the millennial reign of Christ (Rev. 20). After the rapture, multitudes are saved (tribulation saints) through the preaching of the one-hundred-forty-four-thousand, along with the two witnesses (Rev. 5, 7, 11, 14). Many, being Jewish believers, will enter the millennium at the end of the tribulation and after the judgment of the nations (Matt. 25). In comparison, the post-tribulation view suggests the rapture and the second coming happen simultaneously (at the end of the tribulation). This means whoever is left, which cannot include regenerated believers because they have been "caught up" together with Christ, is supposed to immediately return to the earth with Christ. This is a major problem. During the

tribulation, one quarter of the population will die (Rev. 6:8). One third of the population will die later (Rev. 9:18). Many of the population on the earth will perish. One can conclude that only about half of the people will be left on earth. If the church is raptured at the end of the tribulation and then Christ comes to earth in His second coming to destroy those who are left who follow the Antichrist, who then will go into the millennium to repopulate humanity when those who were raptured have glorified bodies? The post-tribulation view leaves many questions unanswered.

5. It distinguishes the church from Israel. God has a plan for His church, which began on the day of Pentecost as recorded in Acts Chapter Two. The church is now waiting for the rapture (1 Thess. 4:13-18; 1 Cor. 15:52-58; Titus 2:11-14). After the rapture, the Judgment Seat of Christ (2 Cor. 5:10; 1 Cor. 3:11-15; Rom. 14:10-12) and the marriage of the Lamb (bridegroom–Rev. 19:7-9) will take place in heaven. Then, Christ will return to the earth with His saints (the church-Rev. 19:11-16) to set up His earthly kingdom (Rev. 20:1-10). At the conclusion of the one thousand years, a new heaven and a new earth will be formed (Rev. 21:1; 2 Pet. 3:10-14). The New Jerusalem described in Revelation 21-22, will be the final destination for the church with access to the new earth. God also has a plan for Israel as shown in His covenants (Abrahamic–Gen. 12-15; Davidic–2 Sam. 7:14-16; Land–Deut. 30, and New–Jer. 31).

6. It differentiates between the passages of Scripture that describe two different events, namely the rapture and the second coming. A careful investigation of the text shows each purpose intended. First, Paul wrote concerning the catching away, or the rapture, in 1 Thessalonians 4:16-18. These verses conclude with "comfort one another with these words." No mention or hint of God's judgment or wrath is made, only consolation and comfort. How can this be explained? John wrote in Revelation 19:11-16:

> And I saw heaven opened, and behold a white horse; ... And the armies *which were* in heaven followed him upon white horses, clothed in fine linen, white and clean. And out of his mouth goeth a sharp sword, that with it he should smite the nations: and he shall rule them with a rod of iron: and he treadeth the winepress of the fierceness and wrath of Almighty God.

Notice the words "fierceness and wrath of Almighty God." John is saying when Christ returns this time, it will be a time of judgment. There is no mention of "comfort," but of blood, war, and judgment. How can one reconcile this passage with 1 Thessalonians 4:18, where Paul did not allude to any judgment at all but only mentioned, "comfort one another"? The conclusion is that these are two different events: 1) the rapture, and 2) the return of Christ in glory and power.

7. Another confusing issue with the rapture being placed at the middle or end of the tribulation as opposed to the beginning can be found in the terminology used by Paul and Zechariah. Paul used the phrase "meet the Lord in the air" (1 Thess. 4:16-17) and Zechariah wrote, "his feet shall stand on the mountain of Olives, which is before Jerusalem" (Zech. 14:1-4). Do these events happen at the same time or are they two different events? A closer investigation will reveal the meaning. In 1 Thessalonians 4:16-18, Paul is explaining to the Thessalonians that they will see their loved ones again when Jesus comes in the rapture and they will meet him in the "air." There is no mention of Him coming to the earth. However, Zechariah 14:1-4, reveals that Jesus will literally stand upon the earth:

> Behold, the day of the LORD cometh ... And his feet shall stand in that day upon the mount of Olives, which *is* before Jerusalem on the east, and the mount of Olives shall cleave in the midst thereof toward the east and toward

the west, *and there shall be* a very great valley.

There are several interesting words and phrases in these verses. This time is described as "the day of the Lord," and is a time of judgment. According to prophecy teacher Dr. Jimmy DeYoung, "the day of the Lord" is "any time in history when God intercedes in the affairs of man personally on the earth."[6] Both Isaiah and Joel mention "the day of the Lord" as a time of God's wrath and judgment (Isa. 13:9-10; Joel 1:15, 2:2). "The day of the Lord" is also emphasized in the book of Zephaniah (Zeph. 1:18, 2:3). There is a historical fulfillment in the days of Judah, as well as a prophetical fulfillment to take place in the future during the days of the tribulation (1 Thess. 5:2; 2 Thess. 2:1-4). "The day of the Lord" has two meanings. Generally speaking, it includes one thousand and seven years (the time after the rapture through both the tribulation and the millennial reign of Christ). Specifically speaking, it is the event when Jesus returns to the earth and puts his feet on the Mount of Olives during his second coming (Zech. 14:4; Matt. 24:29-44; Rev. 19:11-16). In Zechariah 14:1-4, "the day of the Lord" is a time when God shall "gather all nations against Jerusalem to battle." Then the Lord will "fight against those nations" on earth—not in the clouds. Thirdly, it is a time of an earthquake that changes the geographical topography of Jerusalem and all of Israel (Ezek. 40-47). This sets the stage for the millennial reign of Christ from his throne in Jerusalem on earth. Therefore, one must conclude that the second coming of Christ (Zech. 14:4) is an event which takes place on earth and is therefore different than the rapture, which takes place in the "air" (1 Thess. 4:16-18).

8. Another issue is the so-called problem with the wording "meet the Lord in the air." According to Greek scholars, the word "meet" is ἀπάντησις, εως, ἡ (ap-an'-tay-sis). It means the act of meeting, or to meet (a phrase seemingly technical for the

---

6 Jimmy DeYoung, "Prophetic Prospective Daily Devotional: Joel 2:28," Prophecy Today, http://devotional.prophecytoday.com/search?q=Joel+2%3A28 (accessed December 23, 2013).

reception of a newly arrived official).⁷ According to Blaising and Moo, the idea is that a delegation goes out from a city to welcome and receive an arriving dignitary.⁸ Post-tribulationists use this verse to refute the pre-tribulation view. Their argument is that this word "meet"—ἀπάντησις—shows the church will be raptured at the end of the tribulation and then come back to the earth with Christ. Post-tribulationists interpret the word to mean a delegation who will go out to meet a dignitary and then return to the city. There are problems with this interpretation. First, the church will go out of a city—caught up—to meet the Lord, but actually, the dead will be raised with the believers here on earth. Secondly, this will be accomplished by a great force—caught up—not by the church's own accord. Third, there is nothing said in the passage about the church returning back to the earth with the one they meet. Rather, it just refers to comforting one another (1 Thess. 4:18). Fourth, there is no mention of a timeframe to the meeting. To insinuate an instant return is to read into the Scriptures (eisegesis, not exegesis). Fifth, the concept of Jesus coming again (both the rapture and second coming) is in two phases. He comes back for the church and then with the church (1 Thess. 4:16-17; Rev. 19:14).

9. It clarifies the pre-wrath view of trying to identify 1 Thessalonians 4, with Matthew 24:31. Where are the major signs included in the rapture, "comfort one another" comparing "immediately after the days of tribulation … the sun etc., misunderstanding of the word "tribulation."⁹

10. Those who are saved during the tribulation will be considered tribulation saints, not the church (Rev. 6).¹⁰

11. It includes the signs during the tribulation (Matt. 24:15; Dan. 9:27), i.e., the Abomination of Desolation which both Daniel

---

7   Blue Letter Bible, "G-529 – apantesis – Strong's Greek Lexicon (KJV)", https://www.blueletterbible.org//lang/lexicon/lexicon.cfm?Strongs=G529&t=KJV (accessed November 13, 2018).
8   Craig A. Blaising and Douglas J. Moo, *Three Views on the Rapture*, 128, 143.
9   Blaising and Moo, *Three Views on the Rapture*, 116.
10   Ibid., 129.

and Jesus spoke about and the leading up to the second coming of Christ which there are no signs (Matt. 24:36).

As one can conclude, these reliable investigations and biblical explanations give ample reasons to trust the pre-tribulation view as the most biblically accurate.

Post-Tribulation (Chronological, Biblical, Practical)

The post-tribulation view has numerous problems concerning the timeframe and chronological events of the Judgment Seat of Christ and the return of Christ with his church as follows (Rev. 19:14):

1. The saints who return with Christ will be clothed in white garments, which describes the righteousness of the saints.
2. This clothing will be part of the wedding garments, which the church will wear at the wedding of the lamb and the wedding supper of the lamb (Rev. 19:7-8).
3. If the church is raptured at the end of the tribulation when Christ comes again, this does not allow any time for the Judgment Seat of Christ to take place, which results in the clothing of the wedding garments because of the righteousness of the saints (1 Cor. 3:11-14; 2 Cor. 5:10; Rev. 19:8, 22:14).
4. If the church is raptured before the tribulation as described in John 14, and then taken to the Father's house, this allows time for the Judgment Seat of Christ to take place in heaven while God's judgment is poured out on earth. At the end of the tribulation, the Church returns with her bridegroom (Eph. 5:25), clothed in her wedding dress (white garments as described in Revelation 19:14).

This chronological problem can be synchronized in the pre-tribulation view. The explanation and investigation verifies the pre-tribulation view as the right interpretation.

Pre-Wrath
(Historical and Prophetical)

The main differences in the pre-tribulation view and the pre-wrath view have to do with the church going through the tribulation as follows:

1. The pre-wrath view teaches the multitude in Revelation 7:9-10 and 15:2-4, is interpreted as the church.[11]
2. The pre-wrath view teaches the multitude in heaven is the church.[12]
3. The pre-wrath view teaches the church will see the abomination of desolation.[13]
4. The pre-wrath view teaches that the wrath of God does not start until midway (five-and-a-half years) through the tribulation with the opening of the sixth seal.[14]
5. The pre-wrath view teaching is a misunderstanding of God's purpose in Daniel's prophecy concerning the 70th week. This was written to the Jews, not the church (Dan. 9:24-27). It included a panoramic view of the end time purposes for the Jewish people; i.e. returning, rebuilding, Messiah cut off, the Antichrist's abomination of desolation, and the final events in the seventieth week.
6. The pre-wrath view creates confusion with the doctrine of imminency (1 Thess. 4:15; 1 Cor. 15:51, 1:7; Titus 2:13; Phil. 3:20-21). The next event is the rapture of the church, which could happen at any moment. The Antichrist does not have to appear first and neither does the abomination need to take place before Jesus comes for His church. Paul uses the word "we." He was looking for the rapture. He did not believe that the rapture would occur after the confirmation of the Antichrist.

---

11   Blaising and Moo, *Three Views on the Rapture*, 130.
12   Ibid., 145.
13   Ibid., 110-111.
14   Ibid., 129.

Response to Pre-Wrath
(Prophetical, Exegetical, Chronological)

Below is an explanation for refuting the pre-wrath view.

1. Technically speaking, Jesus is speaking to the Jewish disciples (Peter, James and John, etc.) in Matthew's Olivet Discourse, not the church (Matt. 24). The church's origin was in Acts 2, fifty days after the resurrection of Jesus. Jesus instructs the disciples about God's plan for them during the tribulation and His second coming (vv. 4-29f). An incorrect interpretation of this Scripture (the pre-wrath view—to say Jesus is talking to the church instead of the Jews) leads one to conclude that the church will go through at least part of the tribulation. This is the mistake of the pre-wrath view.

2. Technically speaking, in Revelation 5:5-7, Jesus is given the scroll to open its contents, which contain the seven seal judgments of God:

> And one of the elders saith unto me, Weep not: behold, the Lion of the tribe of Judah, the Root of David, hath prevailed to open the book, and to loose the seven seals thereof. And I beheld, and, lo, in the midst of the throne and of the four beasts, and in the midst of the elders, stood a Lamb as it had been slain, having seven horns and seven eyes, which are the seven Spirits of God sent forth into all the earth. And he came and took the book out of the right hand of him that sat upon the throne.

Jesus takes the scroll from God the Father and opens all the seals, not just the sixth seal. Judgment follows every seal. This is not the devil's judgment as the pre-wrath teaches, but rather this is God's judgment. Jesus is the one holding and breaking the seals. "And I saw when the Lamb opened one of the seals …" (Rev. 6:1). Jesus is the Lamb. Neither the devil, nor the Antichrist, is opening the seals (wrath). Jesus is the one, and yet, He is the one that declared to His church, "God's not appointed us to wrath ..." (1 Thess. 5:9). The Bible does not contradict itself. In the midst of the first three-and-a-half years of the tribulation during the opening of the sixth seal by Jesus, John wrote, "For the day of his great wrath is come" (Rev. 6:17). Robert Thomas notes that the words "is come" Greek—eletha—ἔρχομαι is aorist indicative.[15] This means the judgment has already begun (Rev. 6:1f) and is continuing. Those who hold the pre-wrath view claim the judgment begins at the opening of the sixth seal then the church is raptured. However, a grammatical analysis indicates that this is an incorrect conclusion based on proper exegesis. The great multitude that will be saved during the tribulation will be martyred saints, not the church, which will be raptured prior to the tribulation (Rev. 7:9-17).

3. A wrong presupposition leads to a wrong conclusion. "We conclude then that Matthew, Paul, and John all agree that the rapture of the Church will occur after the middle of Daniel's seventieth week."[16]

4. An inference then follows that the church will see the Antichrist, according to Matthew and Paul. However, Paul wrote in 2 Thessalonians 2:1-2, in regards to the "day of the Lord" and the revealing of the Antichrist, "man of sin":

> Now we beseech you, brethren, by the coming of our Lord Jesus Christ, and by our gathering together unto him, That ye be not soon shaken in mind, or be troubled, neither by spirit, nor by word, nor by letter as from us, as that the day of Christ is at hand.

However, according to this author, a closer look at the phrase, "the coming of our Lord Jesus Christ and by our gathering together unto

---

15 Blaising and Moo, *Three Views on the Rapture*, 61.
16 Ibid., 141.

him," gives some insight as to the timing of these events and how they relate to the "day of the Lord."

First, the phrase "the coming of our Lord Jesus" is the Greek word παρουσία (pronounced par-oo-see'-ah).[17] Parousia is used interchangeably with the words epiphany (to bring forth) and apokalupsis (to reveal). According to Charles Fienberg, the word apokalupsis is found eighteen times in the New Testament, epiphany is found six times, and parousia is found twenty-four times. Epiphaneia has three meanings in a total of six passages as follows:[18]

1. the first advent of Christ (2 Tim. 1:10)
2. the rapture (1 Tim. 6:14; 2 Tim. 4:1, 8; Titus 2:13)
3. the revelation (2 Thess. 2:8)

Parousia has three different usages:

1. any coming or anyone's presence (Stephanus and Fortunatus–1 Cor. 16:17; 2 Cor.–10:10; Phil. 1:26; 2:12; Antichrist-Christ–2 Thess. 2:9, etc.)
2. the day of God (2 Pet. 3:12)
3. the rapture (1 Cor. 15:23; 1 Thess. 2:19; 4:15; 5:23; 2 Thess. 2:1; James 5:7-8; 2 Pet. 1:16; 3:4; 1 John 2:28)
4. the revelation (Matt. 24:3, 27, 37, 39; 1 Thess. 3:13; 2 Thess. 2:8)

One concludes there is insufficient evidence based on the study of Greek words in relation to the second coming of Christ with His saints and for His saints.

Second, the phrase "our gathering together unto him" is the Greek word ἐπισυναγωγή.[19] J. Vernon McGee states this verse is a reference

---

17 Blue Letter Bible, "G-3952 – parousias – Strong's Greek Lexicon (KJV)", https://www.blueletterbible.org//lang/lexicon/lexicon.cfm?Strongs=G3952&t=KJV (accessed November 13, 2018).
18 Charles L. Feinberg, *Millennialism*, 286-287.
19 Blue Letter Bible, "G-1997 – episunagoge – Strong's Greek Lexicon (KJV)", https://www.blueletterbible.org//lang/lexicon/lexicon.cfm?Strongs=G1997&t=KJV (accessed November 13, 2018).

to the rapture.[20] The rapture precedes the "day of the Lord" and the revealing of the "man of sin." However, something else is mentioned that comes before the "day of the Lord." What is it?

> Let no man deceive you by any means: for *that day shall not come*, except there come a falling away first, and that man of sin be revealed, the son of perdition; who opposeth and exalteth himself above all that is called God, or that is worshipped; so that he as God sitteth in the temple of God, shewing himself that he is God. Remember ye not, that, when I was yet with you, I told you these things? (2 Thess. 2:3-5).

Third, that day (day of the Lord) shall not come until a "falling away." The Greek word for "falling away" is ἀποστασία (ap-os-tas-ee'-ah).[21] A short definition is defection, apostasy. There are different interpretations for this apostasy. The Wycliffe, Coverdale, and Tyndale all translate the word as a "departure." [22] Therefore, some scholars teach that this is the rapture of the church. Others such as F.F. Bruce see the word to mean a political and spiritual "falling away."[23] Either way, this does not diminish the entire pre-tribulation view in the text or context.

> And now ye know what withholdeth that he might be revealed in his time. For the mystery of iniquity doth already work: only he who now letteth *will let*, until he be taken out of the way. And then shall that Wicked be revealed, whom the Lord shall consume with the spirit of his mouth, and shall destroy with the brightness of his coming: *Even him*, whose coming is

---

20   J. Vernon McGee, *Thru the Bible*, vol. 5 (Nashville, TN: Thomas Nelson, 1983), 412.
21   Blue Letter Bible, "G-646 –apostasia – Strong's Greek Lexicon (KJV)", https://www.blueletterbible.org//lang/lexicon/lexicon.cfm?Strongs=G646&t=KJV (accessed November 13, 2018).
22   Tim LaHaye, Thomas Ice, and Ed Hindson, eds., The Popular Handbook on the Rapture (Eugene, OR: Harvest House Publishers, 2011), 169-170.
23   F.F. Bruce, *Word Biblical Commentary*, vol. 45 (Waco, TX: Word Books Pub., 1982), 166-167.

after the working of Satan with all power and signs and lying wonders, And with all deceivableness of unrighteousness in them that perish (2 Thess. 2:6-9).

Fourth, the restrainer must be taken away and the man of sin revealed. Who is the restrainer? The Holy Spirit is holding back the Antichrist through the church. Being the third person of the trinity, even though the church will be removed, the omnipresent God —the Holy Spirit—will remain. What starts the tribulation? It is not the event of the rapture, but rather the "confirming of the covenant" (Dan. 9:27). This will happen shortly after the rapture of the church. There is something holding the Antichrist back.

The pre-wrath view states that "the day of Christ" is included in the rapture.[24] Furthermore, in order for this view to be consistent with this exegesis, this infers "the day of the Lord" will overtake believers since they will go through one half of the tribulation.

> Let no man deceive you by any means: for *that day shall not come*, except there come a falling away first, and that man of sin be revealed, the son of perdition; who opposeth and exalteth himself above all that is called God, or that is worshipped; so that he as God sitteth in the temple of God, shewing himself that he is God. Remember ye not, that, when I was yet with you, I told you these things? And now ye know what withholdeth that he might be revealed in his time. For the mystery of iniquity doth already work: only he who now letteth *will let*, until he be taken out of the way. And then shall that Wicked be revealed, whom the Lord shall consume with the spirit of his mouth, and shall destroy with the brightness of his coming: *Even him*, whose coming is after the working of Satan with all power and signs and lying wonders, and with all deceivableness of unrighteousness in them that perish; because they received not

---

24   Craig A. Blaising and Douglas J. Moo. *Three Views on the Rapture*, 119.

the love of the truth, that they might be saved. And for this cause God shall send them strong delusion, that they should believe a lie: That they all might be damned who believed not the truth, but had pleasure in unrighteousness (2 Thess. 2:3-12).

From an exegetical, grammatical, chronological, and doctrinal perspective, it becomes apparent the pre-wrath view has some irreconcilable problems. Therefore, the proper and most reliable interpretation points to the pre-tribulation view.

One of the reasons some post-tribulationists reject the pre-tribulation view is because they claim it was not taught until the late 1800's, when it was discovered by John Darby. Supposedly, Darby received the revelation from a young woman named Margaret McDonald who prophesied over a few days, revealing this new doctrine to him. However, Paul Wilkinson pointed out the error of this theory in his scholarly dissertation on Darby.[25]

Bible prophecy teacher, Grant Jeffrey, researched the early church fathers to document their teaching concerning the rapture of the church prior to the tribulation. He discovered several early writers, following the New Testament writers, who taught the doctrine of the imminency of the rapture. He wrote, "Many contemporary writers claim that the pre-tribulation rapture theory first originated around A.D. 1820. They ascribe the theory's initial creation to either Emmanuel Acurnza (Ben Ezra, 1812), Edward Irving (1816), or Margaret Macdonald (1830), and finally to John Darby (1830)."[26] He listed the early Church fathers who wrote:

> For all the saints and Elect of God are gathered, prior to the Tribulation that is to come, and are taken to the Lord lest they see the confusion that is to overwhelm the world because of our sins (On the Last Times, the Antichrist, and the End of the World, by Ephraem the

---

25   Paul Wilkinson and Thomas Ice, "Response to Left Behind or Led Astray," Pre-Trib Research Center, https://www.youtube.com/watch?v=HLWMOdLlSiI (accessed November 13, 2018).

26   Grant Jeffrey, "Rapture: Three Fascinating Discoveries," Pretribulation Rapture, http://www.pretribulation.com/tag/grant-jeffrey (accessed November 13, 2018).

Syrian, A.D. 373).[27]

> Ephraem's manuscript lays out the events of the last days in chronological sequence. Significantly, he began with the Rapture, using the word "imminent," then he described the Great Tribulation of three and a half years duration under the Antichrist's tyranny, followed by the second coming of Christ to earth with His saints to defeat the Antichrist.[28]

Then, Jeffrey quoted John Gill, a Baptist preacher writing in 1748, concerning the events of the rapture prior to the tribulation and the second coming of Christ.

> The Apostle, having something new and extraordinary to deliver concerning the coming of Christ, the first resurrection, or the resurrection of the saints, the change of the living saints and the Rapture both of the raised, and living in the clouds to meet Christ in the air expresses itself in this manner.[29]

"Then we which are alive and remain shall be caught up together with them in the clouds, to meet the Lord in the air; and so shall we ever be with the Lord" (I Thess. 4:17). In commenting on this verse, Gill revealed that he understood there would be an interval of time between the rapture and the return of saints with Christ at Armageddon.[30] This historical evidence reveals the doctrine of the rapture of the church long before John Darby. It is another reason to believe the pre-tribulation view is the most reliable view.

---

[27] Grant Jeffrey, "Rapture: Three Fascinating Discoveries," Pretribulation Rapture, http://www.pretribulation.com/tag/grant-jeffrey (accessed November 13, 2018).
[28] Ibid.
[29] Ibid.
[30] Ibid.

Pre-Tribulation (Chronological and Exegetical)

According to a study of the Scriptures, the rapture will take place before the tribulation. Thus, the church does not go through the tribulation. John wrote to the church of Philadelphia, "Because thou hast kept the word of my patience, I also will keep thee from the hour of temptation, which shall come upon all the world, to try them that dwell upon the earth" (Rev. 3:10). Notice that John stated this trial would come upon "all the world." In addition, God's promise is to "keep" the church "from" this terrible time. The word "from" is the word ἐκ which is a preposition that means "out of, from."[31] In other words, God is saying He will keep His church "out of–from" the tribulation.

Comparing Scripture with Scripture also reveals this same literal interpretation. Paul wrote to the Thessalonians in the context of the day of the Lord and the second coming of Christ, not the rapture, "For God hath not appointed us to wrath, but to obtain salvation by our Lord Jesus Christ" (1 Thess. 5:9). God's wrath will be poured out during the tribulation upon those who follow the beast and do not repent (see wrath of the lamb–Rev. 6:16-17). God's wrath will not be for the church. Another text indicates this truth. Paul wrote to the Church of Thessalonica, "For they themselves shew of us what manner of entering in we had unto you, and how ye turned to God from idols to serve the living and true God; and to wait for his Son from heaven, whom he raised from the dead, even Jesus, which delivered us from the wrath to come" (1 Thess. 1:9-10).

In conclusion, according to Scripture, God's wrath, which is to be poured out during the tribulation, is not meant for the church. There is a difference between the wrath of God and the chastisement of God. God does discipline his people, but He does not execute His wrath upon them. The pre-tribulation view is the only view that lines up under this teaching.

---

31   Blue Letter Bible, "G-1537 – ek – Strong's Greek Lexicon (KJV)", https://www.blueletterbible.org//lang/lexicon/lexicon.cfm?Strongs=G1537&t=KJV (accessed November 13, 2018).

Pre-Tribulation (Prophetical)

Still another evidence that the church will be raptured before the tribulation can be found in examining the tribulation period from Revelation, Chapters Six through Eighteen. There is no mention of the word "church" (ἐκκλησία–from ἔκκλητος, called out or forth, and this from ἐκκαλέω); properly, a gathering of citizens called out from their homes into some public place; an assembly.[32] Contrary to Grudem and Ladd's assessment, Israel is not the church regardless of their connection of the meaning of the word "gathering" in both the Old and New Testaments. However, the word church appears both before and after the tribulation in Revelation Chapters 1, 2, and 3, as well as Revelation 22:16.

Even though this is an argument from silence, it is another reason to embrace the pre-tribulation view as the correct interpretation of Scripture. In *Revelation: A Chronology*, DeYoung notes that the word Israel is used thirty times in the book of Revelation:[33]

- 3 times before Revelation 4:1
- 1 time after Revelation 19:11
- 26 times in Revelation 6-19

Over eighty-five percent of the time, Israel is mentioned in chapters six through nineteen, which describe the tribulation period. Why? The answer is because one purpose of the tribulation is to evangelize the Jews (Rev. 7, 14).

To insinuate the church goes through the tribulation is to miss the mark of the purpose of the tribulation. Evangelization of the Jews (Rev. 5, 7), ending the times of the Gentiles (Dan. 2; Luke 21:24), an overthrow of the satanic trinity (Rev. 20:10), and preparing the earth dwellers to receive God's kingdom are all God's purposes for the tribulation. The word church is used 25 times:

---

32 Blue Letter Bible, "G-1577 – ekklesia– Strong's Greek Lexicon (KJV)", https://www.blueletterbible.org//lang/lexicon/lexicon.cfm?Strongs=G1577&t=KJV (accessed November 13, 2018).

33 Jimmy DeYoung, *Revelation: A Chronology* (Nashville, TN: Shofar Communications, 2010, 38-39.

- 19 times in Revelation 1-3
- 6 times after Revelation 19

This is another indicator that the pre-tribulation view adequately explains this observation. Unlike the pre-wrath or post-tribulation view, the pre-tribulation view fits this pattern.

Pre-Tribulation (Grammatical and Hermeneutical)

With precise accuracy, the words of the book of Revelation, Chapter Four, cover these areas. Revelation 4:1-2 states:

> After this I looked, and, behold, a door *was* opened in heaven: and the first voice which I heard *was* as it were of a trumpet talking with me; which said, Come up hither, and I will shew thee things which must be hereafter. And immediately I was in the spirit: and, behold, a throne was set in heaven, and *one* sat on the throne.

The words "after this" are the Greek words μετά, οὗτος, αὕτη, τοῦτο.[34] Chronologically speaking, the Spirit of God is preparing the reader for what is to come after the church age (Rev. 2-3). This is a picture of the rapture of the church. Chapter Two and Three are letters to the seven churches. After the church age (Rev. 2-3), comes the rapture. Chapter Four and Five are a description of John's translation to heaven (Rev. 4-5). Chapter Six begins the wrath of God in the opening of the seal judgments followed by the trumpet and vial, which is during the tribulation—the day of the Lord.

However, in Chapter Four of Revelation, the believer is admonished to stop and look for the "opened door in heaven," and then to listen for "the voice" which will call, "Come up hither." Notice in the

---

34 Blue Letter Bible, "G-3326 – meta– Strong's Greek Lexicon (KJV)", https://ww.blueletterbible.org//lang/lexicon/lexicon.cfm?Strongs=G3326&t=KJV (accessed November 13, 2018).

context, John mentioned that the voice sounded as if it was a "trumpet" talking. Everyone knows that trumpets do not talk literally. The correct literal, historical method of interpretation of this Scripture recognizes this is apocalyptic literature. Apocalyptic literature uses symbols to reveal truth but uses other Scripture to explain the truth. In this case, there are several passages of Scripture that need to be used to find the real meaning of the text.

First, Paul wrote in 1 Thessalonians 4:16-17, "For the Lord himself shall descend from heaven with a shout, with the voice of the archangel, and with the *trump of God*: and the dead in Christ shall rise first." Clearly, this passage is dealing with the rapture of the church as if it has already been established. Another Scripture can be used in this process of interpretation of apocalyptic literature. The theological term for the study of proper interpretation is called hermeneutics, or the science of interpretation.

Second, writing to the church of Corinth, Paul under the inspiration of the Holy Spirit wrote, "Behold, I shew you a mystery; we shall not all sleep, but we shall all be changed, In a moment, in the twinkling of an eye, at the last *trump*: for the *trumpet shall sound*, and the dead shall be raised incorruptible, and we shall be changed" (1 Cor. 15:51-52). Again, notice the words "trumpet shall sound." This futuristic event is the rapture of the church. The conclusion of this study leads one to return to the original passage in Revelation 4:1.

Other Scriptures that have been used to find the correct approach for interpreting the talking trumpet are in the context of the rapture of the church. Therefore, the passage in Revelation 4:1 is a description of what is going to take place when the church is "caught up."

This chronological study of the first four chapters of the book of Revelation reveals the timing of the rapture and confirms the pre-tribulation view.

Pre-Tribulation (Practical and Historical)

John 14:1-3 states:

> Let not your heart be troubled: ye believe in God,

believe also in me. In my Father's house are many mansions: if it were not so, I would have told you. I go to prepare a place for you. And if I go and prepare a place for you, I will come again, and receive you unto myself; that where I am, there ye may be also.

Bible scholars such as John Walvoord, Harry Ironside, William Newell, and Jimmy DeYoung concurred that the Jewish marriage consisted of several parts. First, there was the betrothal period (Deut. 20:7), which would last a year before the actual wedding. Walvoord noted that this part, called the marriage contract, was established and paid for by the groom or his parents because the parties to the wedding were young and had not reached a responsible age.

By analogy, Jesus left heaven to come to earth. By living a life without sin and dying a death in the place of sin, He sacrificially paid the price for His bride, the church. With His own blood, He purchased her (Acts 20:28).

Paul likens the church to the bride of Christ (Eph. 5:23-32). With this in mind, one can picture the bride and groom, after making the contract, departing from each other and going their separate ways until the appointed time. On the one hand, the groom goes back to his father's house to prepare a place for his bride. Jesus said those exact words to His disciples (John 14:1-3), and He ascended to go back to His Father's house where He is right now. Meanwhile, the groom would prepare at the proper time—unannounced—to go back and get his bride. The bride would watch and wait for her bridegroom to return for her. She must be ready.

When the Father would say to his son, "It's time. Son, go get your bride!" Starting with the wedding procession at the father's house, the groom with his escorts would march toward his bride's home shouting, "Behold the bride groom cometh!" Echoing all the way to the bride's home, her bridesmaids would be alerted. Even though it may be at midnight, the bride must be ready and watching every moment with eager anticipation. What a beautiful picture of the church waiting for her bridegroom.

By analogy and at an unannounced time, Jesus, the bridegroom of the church will send forth an escort. "The Lord will descend from heaven with a shout and the voice of the archangel and the trump of God" (1 Thess. 4:16). He will return for His bride. "I will come again."

The Jewish bride would make herself ready and go out to meet her groom. By analogy, the church, the bride of Christ will go out to meet her groom in the air (1 Thess. 4:17). After uniting, the Jewish bride and the groom would go to the father's house for seven days in hiding to consummate the marriage. According to Renald Showers, *The Jewish Encyclopedia* describes the scene of the bride and groom hiding for seven days in the bridal chamber. By analogy, Jesus takes His bride, the church, back to His father's house in hiding for seven years (at judgment seat and marriage). At the end of the seven years, in His second coming, Jesus comes back with His bride who is clothed in her righteous garments.

There is a beautiful parallel between not only Jesus and His bride, which is the church, but also between husbands and wives as depicted in Ephesians Chapter Five and Colossians Chapter Three. According to Paul's letter to the Ephesians, this heavenly relationship, which exists between Jesus and His church, is compared with husbands and wives. Thus, the practical aspect of the righteous acts of the saints on earth—the church—will be revealed later in heaven as she is dressed in fine linen at the marriage to her Groom, namely Jesus. This can also be seen in an earthly marriage by the way each spouse relates to the other. Revelation 19:7-8 states, "Let us be glad and rejoice, and give honour to him: for the marriage of the Lamb is come, and his wife hath made herself ready. And to her was granted that she should be arrayed in fine linen, clean and white: for the fine linen is the righteousness of saints."

At a later time, when the couple became responsible, the wedding ceremony took place. Finally, the marriage supper celebrated the consummation of the marriage. According to Steve Herzig, author of *Jewish Custom and Culture*, the Talmud gives details and guidelines for the ceremony. Herzig commented, "Long ago, a year separated the betrothal from the consummation, allowing the groom to prepare the home and the bride to validate her virginity. Today, these stages are combined into one ceremony called kiddushin."[35]

---

35   Herzig, Steve, *Jewish Culture and Customs* (Bellmawr, NJ: The Friends of Israel, 1997), 55.

Jesus told His disciples that He would take them to His "father's house" (John 14:1-3). These words debunk the idea that the church will be raptured at the end of the tribulation. If the church is raptured at the conclusion of the tribulation, she will immediately return to the earth at the second coming of Christ instead of going to His Father's house. This becomes a chronological and practical evidence in favor of the pre-tribulation view.

Regardless of the overwhelming evidence, there are those like Grudem and Ladd who teach the church is presently in the kingdom. Grudem writes, "It seems best to conclude, with the great majority of the church throughout history that the church will go through the time of tribulation predicted by Jesus."[36] His argument against the pre-tribulation view is fourfold.[37]

1. He says the suffering during the tribulation because of the wrath of God will not affect Christians—Gentiles or Jews, but they will suffer because of persecution. (This is a stretch because the Scripture does not indicate first of all that Christians will be on earth, and second that they will not experience God's wrath—the 144,000 Israelites are said to be spared—but in fact many, if not all, will be martyred who do not worship the beast or his image, see Rev. 20:4).

2. His response to Rev. 3:10 is that this promise to keep "from" is only to one church Philadelphia and not to all the churches. According to him, this most likely refers to the time of suffering and persecution that would come upon the Roman Empire or the inhabited world. The church of Philadelphia would be "guarded" from harm but not taken out of the world. (This fits in the covenant theological system but is not consistent with other Scripture—Kingdom Now thinking).

3. His response to who will or will not be entering the millennium (in glorified bodies—pre-tribulation view) is that when Christ comes again at the end of the tribulation and makes war, he will defeat all the forces, but will not kill or annihilate

---

36   Grudem, 1135.
37   Ibid.

all of them. (It is difficult to imagine that when the blood is said to flow at the horses bridle and He shall "smite the nations," all of the Antichrist's armies and those who come against Jesus Christ will be spared [Rev. 14:19-20, 19:15]. This is inconsistent with other Scripture).

4. His response to the imminency factor is that the signs listed in Matthew 24, i.e., false Christ, wars, preaching the gospel (Matt. 24:14), and the rising of the man of lawlessness have all already happened. (He admits that the signs in the heaven–stars, sun, moon–Matt. 24:29, have not happened but could in just a few minutes prior to Jesus' return).[38]

Grudem adds to his list what he believes to be a more fundamental concern regarding the pre-tribulationist (he is post-trib). It is the (pre-trib) concern to keep the distinction between Israel on earth and the church in heaven. He writes, "The New Testament does not support a distinction of this kind between Israel and the church. Hence it does not imply a need to see a distinction between these groups at the time of the tribulation and the millennium."[39]

However, key verses in both the Old and New Testament reveal the timing of this "end time event" called the rapture (see 1 Cor. 15:20-28, 52-58; John 14:1-3; 1 Thess. 5:1-9; 2 Thess. 2:1-12; Titus 2:11-14; Rev. 3:10; 4:1-2; 6-19). These verses should be examined in their proper context (considering the verses before and after, the entire book, and their comparison with the whole Bible). In order to come to a better understanding of the timing of this event, one must also study the second coming of Jesus Christ and the day of the Lord (Matt. 24; Rev. 19; Dan. 9; Zech. 12-14; Joel 2; Zeph. 1-2).

In summary, despite all the opposition, when all of the evidence is accumulated, it appears to heavily support the church not being in the kingdom at the present time, but rather awaiting the rapture of the church. This does not mean the church is not going through persecution and tribulation on the earth at the present time, even to the point of suffering. However, it does mean the Lord has a purpose and plan for both the church in the rapture and Israel in the tribulation.

---

38 Grudem, 1101-1105.
39 Ibid., 1133.

Questions for Review and Discussion

1. What does the word "rapture" mean? Where is the key Scriptural reference for the teaching of the rapture?
2. Name the four different views in relation to the timing of the rapture.
3. Describe each view briefly.
4. List some reasons for supporting the pre-trib view.
5. Discuss the passage Paul wrote in 2 Thessalonians 2:1-12.
6. What are the reasons some reject the pre-trib view?
7. Give biblical references that support the pre-trib view.

Chapter Four

The King's Preservation of the Church Before the Kingdom (Revelation 2-3)

If the church is not in the kingdom now, then what is Jesus' purpose and plan for His bride? Conversely, if the church is in the kingdom now according to Grudem and others, then how does that affect God's plan? Is the church supposed to be militant and facilitate a government takeover that will ultimately lead to the second coming of Christ? If one rejects the Dominionism view of the church (the church is facilitating a governmental takeover from a Christian perspective then Christ comes again), then does that mean the church is weak and anemic? Has the church been given the keys to the kingdom for the present or is this meant for the kingdom to come in the future?

The word church is used only two times in the gospels (Matt. 16:18, 18:17). Jesus says in response to Peter, "Upon this rock I will build my church; and the gates of hell shall not prevail against it. And I will give unto thee the keys of the kingdom of heaven: and whatsoever thou shalt bind on earth shall be bound in heaven: and whatsoever thou shalt loose on earth shalt be loosed in heaven" (Matt. 16:18-19). Rather than building His church upon Peter, the correct translation is that His church would be built on the confession of Peter. "Thou art the Christ, the Son of the living God" (Matt. 16:16).

There are several reasons to come to this conclusion. First, the Lord could have said He would build upon "you" to Peter as some have suggested but instead He said upon "this" rock. Blomberg writes, "There is obviously nothing in these verses of the distinctively Catholic doctrines of the papacy, apostolic succession, or Petrine infallibility or of the Protestant penchant for Christian personality cults."[1] He refutes the idea that the church is built upon Peter by saying, "A distinction between 'Peter' and 'this rock' is often affirmed on the basis of the two different Greek words. But grammar requires this variation because the ending of *petra* (rock) is feminine and could not be used for a man's name."[2]

Second, as Toussaint points out, the name Peter is not *petra* (ledge or a mass of rock) but *petros* (a stone).[3] He goes on to say, "What the Lord designated by this term was something entirely new, an organism which had never before had existence nor was even conceived … Christ calls it my church … The Lord certainly could not say of Israel 'My church.'"[4] The church is not built on Peter, nor is it the new Israel.

In order to derive that conclusion (that the church is Israel), one must read into the Scriptures allegorically and thus spiritualize the Old Testament promises to Abraham, David, and the nation of Israel. Instead, a literal reading of the text means God is actually promising Israel certain things He will do. Presently, those promises have not all been fulfilled (Land Covenant—all the land in Deut. 30). Therefore, that means if God is true to His Word, future fulfillments can be expected, which will take place in the kingdom period. Before God will take back His promises, Jeremiah says, "thus saith the Lord; if ye can break my covenant of the day, and my covenant of the night, and that there should not be the day and night in their season, Then may also my covenant be broken with David my servant, that he should not have a son to reign upon his throne" (Jer. 33:19-21). Jeremiah is saying the sun and moon will cease to shine if God takes back His promise.

And yet in the mind of God, He chose to send His Son to take

---

1 Blomberg, 256.
2 Ibid., 252.
3 Toussaint, 202.
4 Ibid., 203.

away sins once and for all (Heb. 8-10), and give humanity (including the Jewish people) an opportunity to be in a right relationship with Him through the shedding of blood (Lev. 17:11; Heb. 9:22; Eph. 1:7; 1 Pet. 1:18-19; Rev. 1:5) and by placing their faith in Him. Because of the death, burial, resurrection, and ascension of Jesus Christ (1 Cor. 15:3-4; Rom. 4:25; 1 Pet 2:21-24; 2 Cor. 5:21), which the Old Testament prophets prophesied (Isa. 53:4-6: Isa. 9:6-7), man is forgiven of his sins (Rom. 3:23; 5:8; 6:23). By trusting and calling upon Jesus alone, without good works (Eph. 2:8-9; Titus 3:5-6), man is restored back into fellowship with his Creator (Rom. 10:9-17) and united with the church. The church is comprised of believers who are to carry out His redemptive plan until He comes again. Following this, the church is established on earth before the kingdom period for the purpose of fulfilling God's will and glorifying Him. In addition, His will for the church (believers) is to be conformed to His image (Rom. 8:29-30) by the power of the Holy Spirit and to proclaim the gospel, as well as live out the Spirit—filled life (Eph. 5:18). All of this is in preparation for when the church will be "caught up" in the clouds to meet the Lord in the air and then appear before the Judgment Seat of Christ (2 Cor. 5:10). God has delegated this authority to His church.

When commenting about Matthew 16:19, concerning the keys to the kingdom, Vlach writes, "Because Jesus mentions the 'church' in close proximity to His statements about the kingdom, some identify the church as the kingdom of heaven, but the two are distinct although related concepts."[5] The debate is between the kingdom now teaching for the church or the kingdom later during the millennium. The correct interpretation brings out the right understanding.

Evans argues against Vlach's view by saying, "Jesus said the church He's building will have the keys to the kingdom of God, giving it the authority to bind and loose on earth and in heaven."[6] According to Evans, "The keys to the kingdom are the church's authority to make disciples and call people out of darkness and into light in Jesus's name. Binding and loosing refer to the church's authority in the world to bring about God's kingdom rule."[7] Once a Bible teacher commits

---

5   Vlach, 338.
6   Evans, *Kingdom Disciples*, 152.
7   Ibid.

to the concepts of the church being in the kingdom now, all other passages of Scripture must be interpreted from that slant in order to fit into that theological system.

However, Toussaint counters Evans by saying, "While many commentators do not identify the kingdom of verse nineteen with the church of verse eighteen, most attempt to associate them in some way."[8] He explains further, "The Messiah does not promise positions in the church but rather He assures them thrones in the millennial kingdom."[9] He concludes by saying, "Therefore, the verse is a promise to Peter of a place of authority in the future earthly kingdom."[10] In the next chapter of Matthew's gospel, which has already been discussed (Matt. 19:28), Jesus promises Peter the reward of sitting on the twelve thrones to judge the twelve tribes of Israel (not the church).

Ryrie clarifies the dispensational view when he writes,

> Dispensationalists fully recognize that the church is Christ's church (Matt. 16:18). He chose and trained its first leaders during His earthly ministry. Some of His teaching ... the church did not come into functional and operational existence until the Day of Pentecost. It is distinctive to this time.[11]

While the church is in the process of becoming more like Christ, there remains a good bit of work to do. After evaluating nineteen centuries of church history, McClain explains, "The church must be perfected in order to reign with Christ over the nations in the coming Kingdom (Rom. 8:17-23)."[12]

The Kingdom in the Epistles of Paul

Paul uses the word kingdom eighteen times in his epistles. In the gospels, it is used one hundred and twenty-one times. The epistles

---

8 Toussaint, 204.
9 Evans, *Kingdom Disciples*, 152.
10 Ibid., 205.
11 Ryrie, *Dispensationalism*, 147.
12 McClain, 330.

references are found in Rom. 14:17; 1 Cor. 4:20, 6:9-10, 15:24, 50; Gal. 5:21; Eph. 5:5; Col. 1:13, 4:11; 1 Thess. 1:5; 2 Tim. 4:1, 18. In each context, it means divine rule. McClain writes, "The theory that Christ and the saints are now reigning in a present kingdom of God on earth, is specifically refuted by the Apostle Paul."[13]

Explaining his position, McClain writes, "Some of these passages assert specifically that the Kingdom belongs to the *future* rather than to the present age of the Church."[14] He goes into more detail by listing several other passages in the epistles that speak of the kingdom as something the church will inherit (1 Cor. 6:9, 10, 15:50; Gal. 5:21; Eph. 5:5; James 2:5).[15]

Most Bible expositors choose not to discuss the terminology "the kingdom of God" in Romans 14:17. This author researched these writers and discovered there were no comments in their commentaries on the subject of the kingdom of God in Romans 14:17 (Newell, Haldane, Moffatt, Phillips, Barclay, Carroll, etc.). While there is an element of truth that pertains to present day living in the church in regards to treating weaker and stronger brothers in Christ, this does not negate the contextual meaning of "the kingdom of God" in relation to the future in a technical sense.

In a sense, the church can be considered in the kingdom of God from the Lord's perspective because of His omniscience. He already sees the kingdom on earth and eternity future. Paul writes with this view in mind (Col. 1:13; Eph. 2:6; 1 Cor. 4:20). By comparison, believers can consider themselves as already "glorified," though technically speaking, believers still have the sinful flesh (Gal. 5:16-24) to battle until they get "glorified bodies" (1 Cor. 15:52-58; 1 John 3:1-3). This event, which is called the rapture, has not happened. However, in the mind of God it has already happened. Paul writes with this language in mind. "For whom he predestined ... called ... justified ... glorified" (Rom. 8:29-30), "If ye be risen with Christ" (Col. 3:1), "Quickened us together and raised us up together to sit in heavenly places in Christ Jesus" (Eph. 2:5-6). Positionally, the believer is already in the kingdom (Col. 1:13) as far as God is concerned (He sees eternity past

---

13   McClain, 433.
14   Ibid., 432.
15   Ibid., 433.

and eternity future). Practically, the kingdom awaits the believer when Christ comes and sets up His kingdom. Therefore, it is confusing to teach the church is in the kingdom now.

Vlach picks up on this theme and quotes Douglas Moo, "Christians are positionally related to the King and His kingdom and are to exhibit kingdom righteousness in their lives. Yet the kingdom and reign of Jesus the Messiah await the future."[16] In response to Colossians 1:13, McClain concurs that the believer has been placed in the kingdom of God. He explains, "In the same sense, we have been (aorist tense) transferred *judicially* into the Kingdom of our Lord even before its establishment."[17] According to Paul's writings, Abraham had faith in God by "calleth those things which be not as though they were" (Rom. 4:17). To say the believer is in the kingdom now literally is where the disagreement occurs.

In 2 Timothy 4:1, Paul mentions the kingdom in the context of Jesus' appearing. Later in 2 Timothy 4:18, he writes, "And the Lord shall deliver me from every evil work, and will preserve *me* unto his heavenly kingdom: to whom *be* glory for ever and ever. Amen." Vlach writes, Farnell is correct that "in the epistles, the dominate teaching of the 'kingdom of God' centers on a future kingdom and not a present one."[18]

Several passages in Paul's letter to the believers in Rome need to be addressed. First, in Romans 14:17, the word "kingdom" is used in the context of Christians judging one another (Rom. 14-15). Paul writes "For the kingdom of God is not meat and drink; but righteousness, and peace, and joy in the Holy Ghost" (Rom. 14:17). Did the word kingdom mean present or future? McClain writes, "The thought here fits a *future* Kingdom better than a present one."[19] He explains about meat and drink for the church now and in the kingdom. "Therefore, since the Church is to reign in that Kingdom, its members should

---

16   Douglas Moo, *The New International Commentary on the New Testament: The Epistles to the Romans* (Grand Rapids, MI: Eerdman, 1996), 857, quoted in Michael J. Vlach, *He Will Reign Forever* (Silverton, OR: Lampion Press, 2017), 40.
17   McClain, 435.
18   David F. Farnell, "The Kingdom of God in the New Testament", The Master's Seminary Journal 23 (2012), 193-208, quoted in Michael J. Vlach, *He Will Reign Forever* (Silverton, OR: Lampion Press, 2017), 433.
19   McClain, 434.

not judge or grieve one another in such matters here and now. All disputes of this nature should be left for the 'Judgment Seat of Christ' which will inaugurate His Kingdom upon the earth (v.10)."[20] In the context of Romans 14:10, Paul writes, "For we shall all stand before the Judgment Seat of Christ." Paul is reminding the believers in Rome, which consisted of both Jews and Gentiles, that the kingdom to come should be the focus of how believers treat one another. This will motivate each one to love and preserve unity in the body of Christ more than food and drink.

Arguing against this view, O'Brien mentions the aorist tenses which point to a past event.[21] Writing on the passage in Romans 14:17, Marvin Vincent agrees, "Not the future, messianic kingdom."[22] In regards to the phrase "the kingdom of God" in Romans 14:17, A.T Robertson writes, "Not the future kingdom of eschatology, but the present spiritual kingdom, the reign of God in the heart, of which Jesus spoke so often."[23] James Dunn, commenting on Romans 14:17, states,

> The thought here is very much of a piece with the eschatological tension so characteristic of Paul's thought – the Spirit, indeed, as the first installment of the inheritance which is the kingdom (1 Cor. 6:9-11; Gal. 4:6-7 also Eph. 1:13-14. For both Jesus and Paul the Spirit is the presence of the kingdom still future in its complete fulfillment ... still future rule of God can provide inspiration and enabling for the present.[24]

F. F. Bruce writing on this passage of Scripture says, "For Paul, 'the kingdom of God' (as distinct from the present kingdom of Christ) is future inheritance of the people of God; but 'in the Holy Ghost' its

---

20   McClain, 434.
21   Peter O'Brien, *Colossians and Philemon*, vol. 44, Word Biblical Commentary (Waco, TX: Word, 1982), 82.
22   Marvin Vincent, *Word Studies in the New Testament*, vol. 1, 2 (Grand Rapids, MI: Eerdman, 1989), 170.
23   Archibald T. Robertson, *Word Pictures in the New Testament*, vol. 4 (Grand Rapids, MI: Baker, 1931), 415.
24   James Dunn, *Word Biblical Commentary*, vol. 38 (Dallas, TX: Word Books, 1988), 822-823.

blessings can be enjoyed already."²⁵ Murray concurs on this passage, "The kingdom of God is that realm to which believers belong."²⁶ While it is apparent, there are differences in the specifics of Romans 14:17 concerning the kingdom of God whether now or in the future, the proper interpretation is the goal rather than approaching the passage with a biased theological system.

There is another passage of Scripture found in Romans 15:12 that is in question. The interpretation leads some to embrace a present Messianic reign of Jesus Christ over the nations. "There shall be a root of Jesse, and he shall rise to reign over the Gentiles; in him shall the Gentiles trust." A closer investigation of the previous verses indicate that Paul is not saying these four promises have been fulfilled (vv. 9-12). Furthermore, going back to verse eight, one reads, "Now I say that Jesus Christ was a minister of the circumcision for the truth of God, to confirm the promises made unto the fathers" (Rom. 15:8). Paul never mentions this was fulfilled when Jesus came the first time. Rather, as McClain points out in verse eight "the verb confirm is (*bebaioo*). And this our Lord did establishing firmly the Old Testament promises of a future Kingdom to Israel at their full face value, both by words and deeds."²⁷ Therefore, this attempt to validate the interpretation as being done, thereby establishing the kingdom in the present, is nullified.

Writing to the church of Corinth, Paul says, "For the kingdom of God is not in word but in power" (1 Cor. 4:20). McClain points out, "To interpret 1 Corinthians 4:20 as a present kingdom of the saints would make Paul contradict what he had already written in verses five and eight."²⁸ He also mentions the Greek word "power" (*dunamis*) is the same word used in Hebrews 6:5 in the context of the "age to come."²⁹ The subject of the "judgment when the Lord comes" is the focus in verse five.

According to Paul, some of the Corinthian believers were "puffed up" with pride (1 Cor. 4:6, 18). They were acting like they were already in the kingdom. Paul identifies himself as desiring to reign with them

---

25   F.F. Bruce, *The Epistle to the Romans* (Grand Rapids, MI: Eerdman, 1971), 252.
26   John Murray, *The Epistle to the Romans* (Grand Rapids, MI: Eerdman, 1997), 193.
27   McClain, 434.
28   Ibid., 435.
29   Ibid.

as kings in the kingdom (1 Cor. 4:8). "Now ye are full, now ye are rich, ye have reigned as kings without us: and I would to God ye did reign, that we also might reign with you." This shows that Paul did not teach them that they were in the kingdom because he anticipated being there as well. Vlach concludes, "While the reign of the Messiah and the saints had not begun yet, Paul possesses the power of the Holy Spirit that can transform his life."[30]

Paul's writing to the Corinthians points toward the kingdom yet to come. In the context of the future, Paul says, "Know ye not that the unrighteous shall not inherit the kingdom of God" (1 Cor. 6:9). The believers in Corinth were involved in lawsuits (1 Cor. 6:1-2), and were being rebuked by Paul (1 Cor. 6:2-8). He expresses his disappointment in them. He informs those Christians to apply practical solutions because of future implications, namely, the kingdom to come. Vlach writes, "This is an opportunity for citizens of the kingdom to apply kingdom principles to their lives now."[31] He explains in more detail, "As Ciampa and Rosner rightly note, 'From the perspective of the everlasting kingdom, the Corinthian litigation is trifling … and totally insignificant.'"[32]

Since Christians are not presently ruling over angels, that puts the idea Paul is presenting into proper perspective. It is in the future kingdom (1 Cor. 6:2-3). Robert Yarbrough comments on the phrase "shall not inherit the kingdom of God" (1 Cor. 6:9-10). "By connecting inheritance with the kingdom, Paul indicates that he is using 'kingdom' in its eschatological sense."[33] In conclusion, Paul's explanation of the kingdom (1 Cor. 6:1-11), reveals that it is future and unbelievers will not inherit the kingdom. However, the principles in the future kingdom should affect the church's present lifestyle in preparation for the kingdom.

The next passage in the epistles to examine is 1 Corinthians 15:23-

---

30   Vlach, 434.
31   Ibid., 435.
32   Roy E. Ciampa and Brian S. Rosner, *The First Letter to the Corinthians*, *The Pillar New Testament Commentary* (Grand Rapids, MI: Eerdmans, 2010), 228, quoted in Michael J. Vlach, *He Will Reign Forever*, (Silverton, OR: Lampion Press, 2017), 435.
33   Robert W. Yarbrough, *The Kingdom of God: Matthew and Revelation*, ed. Christopher Morgan and Robert A. Peterson (Wheaton, IL: Crossway, 2012), 266, quoted in Michael J. Vlach, *He Will Reign Forever* (Silverton, OR: Lampion Press, 2017), 436.

26. According to Paul, there are five reasons Christians need to be ready for the next resurrection.

The first reason believers need to be ready for the next resurrection is because of the *insurmountable evidences* of the first resurrection (1 Cor. 15:1-11). There are three insurmountable evidences. The first evidence is the *transformation* of the believer's life (vv. 1-2). The second evidence is the *inspiration* of the Bible (vv. 3-4). Finally, the third evidence is the *affirmation* of the saved (vv. 5-11).

The second reason believers need to be ready for the next resurrection is because of the *inescapable consequences* of the first resurrection (1 Cor. 15:12-19). There are three inescapable consequences. The first one is dead faith (vv. 12-14). The second consequence is a sealed grave (v. 18). Finally, the third consequence is no hope (v. 19).

The third reason believers need to be ready for the next resurrection is because of the *irrefutable occurrences* of the first resurrection (1 Cor. 15:20-34). Notice the two irrefutable occurrences. First, Jesus won the battle over sin (vv. 20-24), and second, death lost (vv. 25-34).

The fourth reason believers need to be ready for the next resurrection is because of the *inseparable deliverances* of the second resurrection (1 Cor. 15:35-49). The first deliverance is from these earthly bodies that are wearing out (vv. 35-40). The second deliverance is found in the fact that the believer's new heavenly body will last forever (vv. 40-49).

The fifth reason believers need to be ready for the next resurrection is because of the *incomparable assurances* of the second resurrection (1 Cor. 15:50-58). The first assurance is that of the *rapture* (vv. 51-52). The second assurance is the *resurrection* (vv. 53-54).

Finally, how can the Christian get ready for the next resurrection? There are two ways. The first is by *avoiding* the sting of death (v. 55). This is possible by being born again (John 3:1-7). The second way the believer can get ready for the next resurrection is by *abounding* in the work of the Lord (v. 58).

The next resurrection, which has to do with His glorious appearing, is based on the validity of the first resurrection. Every believer has the promise of eternal life with a new glorified body (1 Cor. 15:42-54).

However, much debate continues concerning the passage in 1 Corinthians 15:23-26. Some see a threefold order and an intermediate kingdom.³⁴ From this perspective, Jesus was the first (firstfruits) to be resurrected and the saints will be the next to be resurrected at the rapture, followed by an interval of time (seven years-tribulation). Then, Jesus returns in glory and power (Matt. 24:36-44), followed by the one-thousand-year reign of Christ, and finally the exchange of the eternal kingdom from the Son to the Father. Other scholars teach the "end" is at the millennial when Christ comes again.

The writers who support the postmillennial and amillennial positions both attempt to use this passage in defense of their views. A careful examination of the text reveals insights that debunk their conclusions.

Paul wrote, "But now is Christ risen from the dead, and become the firstfruits of them that slept" (1 Cor. 15:20). He was the "firstfruit," which is the Greek word ἀπαρχή. It means the firstfruits, the earliest crop of the year.³⁵ Jesus was the first one to ever come forth out of the grave never to die again, and lead many that would follow in like manner from His empty tomb. In addition, Paul mentioned, "But every man in his own order: Christ the firstfruits; afterward they that are Christ's at his coming" (1 Cor. 15:23). The word "order" is the Greek word τάγμα, which means rank, division.³⁶ It is a military term. God has an order for every man when it comes to being resurrected in relation to "Christ's coming." His "order" is as follows:

1. Jesus Christ–the "firstfruits" (v. 20)
2. church saints in the rapture (1 Thess. 4:16-17)
3. the Old Testament saints at his second coming–some put that at the beginning of millennial (Dan. 12:1-2)
4. the tribulation saints at the beginning of the millennial (Rev. 20:4)
5. the unsaved at the Great White Throne Judgment (Rev. 20:11-15)

---

34 McClain, 435; Vlach, 437.
35 Blue Letter Bible, "G-536 – firstfruit – Strong's Greek Lexicon (KJV)", https://www.blueletterbible.org//lang/lexicon/lexicon.cfm?Strongs=G536&t=KJV (accessed November 25, 2018).
36 Ibid, "G-5001 – order – Strong's Greek Lexicon (KJV)", https://www.blueletterbible.org//lang/lexicon/lexicon.cfm?Strongs=G5001&t=KJV (accessed November 25, 2018).

Paul explains, "Then cometh the end, when he shall have delivered up the kingdom to God, even the Father; when he shall have put down all rule and all authority and power" (1 Cor. 15:24).

A careful investigation of key words reveals important scenarios found in Bible prophecy. Notice, in 1 Corinthians 15:24, the words "then" and "end" ("Then cometh the end"). Those who interpret this verse claim this is proof for believing Jesus will come in the rapture after the tribulation (post-tribulation view) or even after the millennial (postmillennial view). Rather, the more accurate view is Jesus will come in the rapture (for the church) before the tribulation and His second coming will take place after the seven years of tribulation.

Kenneth Gentry writes, "Paul's resurrection discourse in 1 Corinthians 15 provides us with strong New Testament evidence for the postmillennial hope."[37] According to Gentry, in regards to the resurrection (1 Cor. 15:23-24), it will be a general resurrection of both the righteous and the unrighteous.[38]

Writing from the amillennial view, Robert Strimple explains that the premillennial interpretation of 1 Corinthians 15:23-24 is based on the two adverbs (*epetia* and *eita*) "adverbs of time, denoting sequence."[39] Strimple responds to that interpretation (premillennial), "It must be granted that the adverb *eita* can mark a long interval, just as the adverb *epeita* does indicate a long interval here in verse 23. But either of these 'adverbs of sequence' can also be used in the sense of immediate sequence."[40] Strimple, commenting on verse twenty-four "then" and being an amillennialist says, "The broader context of Paul's letters (and the New Testament generally) shows us that 'the end' cannot be separated from the second coming of Christ."[41] This is opposite of the premillennial view. "The end" means the kingdom (when the Son gives it to the Father) not the second coming. Finally, he explains that when Paul writes about the Son handing over the

---

37   Stanley Gundry and Darrell Bock, *Three Views on the Millennial and Beyond* (Grand Rapids, MI: Zondervan, 1999), 48.
38   Ibid., 49.
39   George Ladd, *Crucial Questions About the Kingdom of God* (Grand Rapids, MI: Eerdmans, 1952), 178, quoted in Stanley Gundry and Darrell Bock, *Three Views on the Millenial and Beyond* (Grand Rapids, MI: Zondervan, 1999), 109.
40   Gundry and Bock, *Three Views on the Millennial and Beyond*, 109.
41   Ibid.

kingdom to the Father (v. 24), he is not contradicting Peter.[42] Peter says, "the eternal kingdom of our Lord and Savior Jesus Christ" (2 Pet 1:11). He is correct on that point.

In refuting Strimple, Blaising writes that Strimple admits that the words *epeita* and *eita* (vv. 23-24) can be long intervals.[43] "The word 'end' *telos* (v. 24) … does not necessarily mean the moment of the Second Coming as we can see in 10:11."[44] Blaising teaches the end is a reference to when the Son hands it back to the Father.

Grudem writes about the two words translated "then" (v. 24) *epeita* and *eita,* "they take the sense 'after that', not the sense 'at the same time.'"[45] He explains,

> Just as there is an interval of time between Christ's resurrection and his second coming when we receive a resurrection body (v. 23), so there is an interval of time between Christ's second coming and the end (v. 24), when Christ delivers the kingdom to God after having reigned for a time and put all his enemies under his feet.[46]

Even though Grudem teaches a post-tribulation coming of the Lord without the rapture before the tribulation, he is correct on the interpretation of the phrase "then."

Vlach writes Jesus is "the first fruits of those who are asleep" (1 Cor. 15:23).[47] Jesus has risen from the dead and so will those who die in Him. Vlach describes this passage (1 Cor. 15:22-24) in three stages: (1) "Christ's the firstfruits," (2) "After that those who are Christ's at His coming," and (3) "Then comes the end."[48] He admits there is not much debate on the first two stages but the last stage "then comes the end" is debatable. Vlach holds the view, along with McClain, that there is an intermediate kingdom after Jesus returns but before the

---

42   Gundry and Bock, *Three Views on the Millenial and Beyond*, 112.
43   Blaising, 150.
44   Ibid., 151.
45   Grudem, 1130.
46   Ibid., 1130.
47   Vlach, 436.
48   Ibid., 437.

eternal state when He hands over the kingdom to God the Father.⁴⁹ As already discussed, there are those who teach "the end" means after Jesus returns that will be the end. There is no intermediate millennial period. Which view is correct?

The word "then" is the Greek word εἶτα⁵⁰ which means afterward and "end" is τέλος⁵¹ which means an end or a purpose. The problem is that 'then comes the end' does not mean, immediately after the second coming of Christ comes the end (1 Cor. 15:23). Rather, the same word "then" is used in the same chapter in verses five and seven. Paul was describing Jesus' appearances to Cephas (Peter) and to James and "then" to all the apostles, but the context shows this was at different times with intervals in between.⁵² Jesus appeared for ten days before His ascension. Therefore, we can conclude the phrase "then cometh the end when he shall have delivered up the kingdom to God, even the Father" (1 Cor. 15:24), does not happen immediately one right after another in sequence. But there is an interval of 1,000 years after Jesus' second coming before the "kingdom is delivered up to his father" (1 Cor. 15:24).

To stay true to the literal interpretation within the context and in comparison to other Scriptures, one can see the fitting together of these New Testament passages, which point to the kingdom later rather than now.

Another controversial passage of Scripture in Paul's epistles is Colossians 1:13. Paul is writing to the church to demonstrate the deity of Christ (Col. 1:14-22; 2:9-10) and that He is sufficient for the believer (Col. 1:6-8, 13-15; 3:1-4). He is also refuting the false teaching of ceremonialism, asceticism, and Gnosticism. Along with his other writings (Eph. 1:3-12; 2:5-6; Rom. 6:6-13; 8:13-27; 13:11-14; Gal. 5:16-24; Phil. 1:6), his goal is for believers to know who they are in Christ, both judicially and practically.

---

49   Vlach, 437.
50   Blue Letter Bible, "G-1534 – eita – Strong's Greek Lexicon (KJV)", https://www.blueletterbible.org//lang/lexicon/lexicon.cfm?Strongs=G1534&t=KJV (accessed November 25, 2018).
51   Ibid., "G-5056 – telos – Strong's Greek Lexicon (KJV)", https://www.blueletterbible.org//lang/lexicon/lexicon.cfm?Strongs=G55056&t=KJV (accessed November 25, 2018).
52   Vlach, 439.

Describing what God has done for each believer in Christ, Paul says, "Who hath delivered us from the kingdom of darkness, and translated us into his dear Son" (Col. 1:13). What does it mean? Is this another proof text that the kingdom is present? Was Paul informing those Christians their position in Christ as he does later in Chapter Three? "If ye then be risen with Christ, seek those things which are above, where Christ sitteth on the right hand of God" (v. 1). Those believers had not actually risen with Christ to heaven rather they were in the church on earth. Paul meant positionally in Christ. God already engrafted them into His death, burial, resurrection, and ascension (Rom. 6:1-11; Eph. 2:1-10). Could this be the same meaning of the kingdom passage in Colossians 1:13?

There are different opinions on the true meaning of this phrase. Richard R. Melick, Jr., writes in his commentary on Colossians, "The kingdom is not a geographical place since the believers did not change location when they changed kingdoms. In Christ, God invaded Satan's territory and delivered people."[53] He differentiates between the phrases "the kingdom of Christ" and the "kingdom of God."

> The kingdom of Christ is an intermediate kingdom which will someday be handed over to the Father … The ultimate state for the believer is the kingdom of God, but God planned for Christ and his kingdom to be the focus in the interval between the cross and the return of Christ. Most of the time … he referred to the kingdom of God.[54]

He concludes his discussion on Colossians 1:13 by explaining, "The kingdom of God is a spiritual dimension rather than physical (Rom. 14:17; 1 Cor. 4:20; 15:50)."[55] Peter T. O'Brien, in his commentary, derives at the same conclusion.[56] Writing on the kingdom verses (Matt. 13; Col. 1:13) from the postmillenialist perspective, Gentry says,

---

53   Richard R. Melick, Jr., *The New American Commentary* (Nashville, TN: Broadman, 1991), 207.
54   Melick, *The New American Commentary*, 207.
55   Ibid.
56   O'Brien, 28.

Because of this, first century Christians proclaimed him as king (Acts 5:31; 17:7; Rev. 1:5) with regal dignity, authority, and power (Eph. 1:22; Phil 2:9). Since that time Christ translates us into his kingdom at our conversion (Col. 1:12-13; 4:11; 1 Thess. 2:12) organizes us as a kingdom (1 Pet. 2:9; Rev. 1:6-9) and mystically seats us with him in rulership" (1 Cor. 3:21-22; Eph. 1:3; 2:6; Col. 3:1).[57]

McClain examines the connection in Paul's writings on the subject of the kingdom of God. He concludes that there are common grammatical evidences that clarify the kingdom now from the kingdom to come. In relation to Colossians 1:13, he writes, "the context here suggests that the action must be regarded as *de jure* rather than *de facto*."[58] Christians have been delivered but still battle against the powers of darkness (Eph. 6:12). He connects the passages in Ephesians 2:6 with Colossians 1:13, which reveal the aorist tense verbs and indicate a transfer "judicially into the kingdom even before its establishment."[59] Listing the passages where the word "kingdom" is used by Paul (Col. 4:11; 1 Thess. 2:12; 2 Thess. 1:5), he explains the Greek preposition *eis* is used in all of these which "may be read with the idea of a future Kingdom."[60] Describing the phrase throne *thronos* of God, he explains this is referring to "a divine Kingdom, occurs four times in the Epistle to the Hebrews, and in no other epistle."[61]

McClain admits there is a sense in which the kingdom of God does exist on earth today, however he says, "Christ rules in the Church … but the nature … is different from that of the Mediatorial Kingdom."[62] His Universal Kingdom is acknowledged, yet according to McClain, there is theological confusion when it comes to the church and the kingdom. He explains,

> It is easy to claim that in the 'present kingdom of grace'

---

57   Gundry and Bock, *Three Views on the Millennial and Beyond*, 38.
58   McClain, 435.
59   Ibid.
60   Ibid., 436.
61   Ibid.
62   Ibid., 437.

> the rule of the saints is wholly 'spiritual', exerted only through moral principles and influence. But practically, once the Church becomes the Kingdom in any realistic theological sense, it is impossible to draw any clear line between principles and their implementation through political and social devises. For the logical implications of a present ecclesiastical kingdom are unmistakable, and historically have always led in only one direction, i.e, political control of the state by the Church.[63]

This seems to be a description of Dominionism Theology.

Ryrie clarifies the different theological positions in regards to the church and the kingdom. He says,

> The amillennialist sees that kingdom as the church ruled by Christ. The covenant premillennialist understands the church as the new Israel but also recognizes the future reign of Christ in the millennial kingdom. Almost all progressive dispensationalists do not say that the church is the new Israel, but they teach that the Davidic/Messianic kingdom has been inaugurated and is now operative with Christ on the throne of David in heaven and will operate on this earth in the future Millennium. The normative dispensationalist also does not see the church as the new Israel but understands the fulfillment of the Davidic kingdom promise not happening now but in the Millennium.[64]

This clarification puts the different theological views in comparison. Ryrie discusses his understanding of the church and the kingdom. "Therefore, when a dispensationalist says that the kingdom is postponed, he is speaking of the Davidic kingdom, but he also affirms the continuing presence of the universal kingdom and the spiritual

---

63   McClain, 438-439.
64   Ryrie, *Dispensationalism*, 182-183.

rule of God in individual hearts today."[65]

The Kingdom in Peter, James, and John

Other New Testament writers besides Paul describe the future kingdom. Both James and Peter do. According to Vlach, James 2:5, being "heirs of the kingdom," "indicates a futuristic view of the kingdom."[66] Yarbrough concurs concerning this passage that James speaks of a future kingdom as Jesus did.[67] Peter writes, "Wherefore, the rather, brethren give diligence to make your calling and election sure: for if you do these things, ye shall never fall: For so an entrance … into the everlasting kingdom of our Lord and Savior Jesus Christ" (2 Pet. 1:10-11). Vlach says, "Peter speaks of the kingdom as future here."[68] Researching the words "kingdom" in relation to the "church" in the New Testament books including the gospels has given conclusive evidence of the postponed but future kingdom and the present work of the church until God's kingdom is inaugurated.

McClain writes, "The last book of the Bible is pre-imminently *The Book of the Kingdom of God* in conflict with, and victory over, the kingdoms of this world."[69] He breaks down the usage of words in the book of Revelation.[70] "Throne" (*thronos*) is used forty-one times; thirty-eight times it refers to the divine kingdom and three times to the satanic kingdom. The word "kingdom" (*basileia*) is used seven times–three times to refer to God's kingdom (1:9), and four times to refer to the kingdom of evil (16:10). "Crown" is used eleven times– eight times *stephanos* refers to Christian believers (2:10), also one time to the white horse (6:2), to Israel (12:1), to demons (9:7), and to the Son of man (14:14). The word *diadema* is used three times; one time it is applied to Jesus (19:12), and one time to Satan (12:3). The word "reign" is mentioned seven times, every time with divine kingdom (5:10). "Power" (*exousia)* is used twenty times and has to

---

65 Ryrie, *Dispensationalism*, 183.
66 Vlach, 468.
67 Yarbrough, *The Kingdom of God*, 150, quoted in Vlach, 468.
68 Vlach, 468.
69 McClain, 442.
70 Ibid.

do with authority rule between two opposing kingdoms (2:26, 13:4). "Rule" (*poimaino*) is listed four times and has to do with the sense of shepherdly government in relation to Christ. The proper interpretation is the result of understanding the words correctly.

John was exiled on the Isle of Patmos during a time of severe persecution when Christians were being martyred because of their faith in Jesus when the revelation of Jesus Christ came unto him (Rev. 1:9). God the Father gave it to God the Son who gave it to the angel who gave it to John (Rev. 1:1). A general outline of the book is found in Revelation 1:19. The older pastor, John, who tradition claims to be the only one of the disciples to survive martyrdom, wrote, "Write the things which thou hast seen, and the things which are, and the things which shall be hereafter" (Rev. 1:19). John sees a past, present, and future implication in this statement.

First, the phrase, "the things which thou hast seen" is a reference to John's incredible encounter with the Lord Jesus who has been glorified (Rev. 1:10-17). Consequently, after seeing, hearing, and being in his glory, John fell as a dead man. He was holding the keys to death and hell! His words were "*I am* he that liveth, and was dead; and, behold, I am alive for evermore, Amen; and have the keys of hell and of death" (Rev. 1:18).

The second phrase from the outline from Revelation 1:19 is "the things which are." This is a reference to both Chapters 2 and 3. Seven churches, which were literal churches, are mentioned: Ephesus, Smyrna, Pergamos, Thyatira, Sardis, Philadelphia, and Laodicea.

In light of the rapture of the church, Jesus' message through John to the seven churches is relevant even for today. Words of commendation, correction, and celebration to the churches can be seen. From repenting and returning, to being persecuted and staying faithful, to practicing and following sound doctrine, to discerning and rebuking false teachers, to watching and strengthening the ministry, to obeying and walking through open doors, and to healing, each church was given a specific evaluation along with a recommendation from Jesus Christ.

The last phrase in Revelation 1:19, "the things which shall be hereafter" has a future tense implication. Chronologically, these events would be covered in Revelation 4-22. Sections of this will be studied in a later chapter.

Just because the Dominionism perspective is not interpreted as the best view, this does not mean the church is overcome by this world. How can the church be overcomers (Rev. 2-3)? Do some believers overcome and are others overcome? At the Judgment Seat, will all be rewarded? Is there a special blessing or privilege for just the believers who are overcomers?

John writes, "Unto him that loved us, and washed us from our sins in his own blood, and hath made us kings and priests unto God and his Father; to him be glory and dominion for ever and ever. Amen. Behold, he cometh with clouds" (Rev. 1:5-7). Vlach says not only are "Christians a kingdom" but also "Jesus' message to the seven churches of Revelation 2-3 reveal information concerning the timing of the kingdom of God."[71] Future promises are given to the churches that persevere under trial.

1. Ephesus: right to eat of the tree of life in the Paradise of God (Rev. 2:7)
2. Smyrna: will not be hurt by the second death (Rev. 2:11)
3. Pergamum: given hidden manna, a white stone, and a new name written on the stone (Rev. 2:17)
4. Thyatira: granted authority and rule over the nations (Rev. 2:26-27)
5. Sardis: clothed in white garments, name in the book of life, and confessed before the Father and the angels (Rev. 3:5-6)
6. Philadelphia: given pillar in the temple of God; the name of God and the New Jerusalem (Rev. 3:12)
7. Laodicea: granted to sit down with Jesus on His throne (Rev. 3:21)

Vlach explains, "Jesus does not tell the churches in operation that the kingdom is their experience."[72]

---

71 Vlach, 475.
72 Ibid., 476.

The Kingdom and Overcomers

John says, "And He that overcometh, and keepeth my works unto the end, to him will I give power over the nations: And he shall rule them with a rod of iron ... as I received of my Father" (Rev. 2:26-27). Vlach writes, "When Jesus returns, members of the church will assist Jesus in His rule over the nations (Rev. 2:26-27; 3:21), which includes cultural and societal matters."[73] In more detail, he says, "But in this age before Jesus comes again, the church's mission is not cultural or societal transformation." Vlach makes an interesting observation. "One reason we can know Messiah's kingdom is future is His people are not ruling the nations yet. Revelation 2-3 refutes the view that Jesus' millennial kingdom is now in effect."[74] He comes to that conclusion based on the fact that Satan is not bound (Rev. 20:1-3) and the saints are not reigning (Rev. 20:4). The opposite is true today. Satan is persecuting churches and Christians, and the saints are suffering. McClain concurs, "All the churches of Revelation 2-3 are pictured as living under the sign, *Till He Comes*."[75]

Joseph Dillow says this is a "Thrilling promise to those Christians who remain faithful to Christ to the end of life" (Rev. 2:26).[76] Jesus speaks of continuing in His word (John 8:31). Speaking on being an "overcomer," he notes, "The Greek word translated "to overcome" is *nikao*. It is found in a legal sense of 'winning one's case.' The noun *nike* means 'victory'. *Nike* was the name of a Greek goddess who is often represented in art as a symbol of personal superiority."[77] Dillow lists the three views of overcomers. First, there is the Arminian view. This view states that if a Christian falls away, then he forfeits his salvation.[78] Second, there is the Experimental Predestinarians view, which sees all true Christians will inevitably overcome. The third view is called the Partakers view.[79] This says the overcomer is a faithful Christian

---

73 Vlach, 541.
74 Ibid., 477.
75 McClain, 447.
76 Dillow, *The Reign of the Servant Kings*, 469.
77 Ibid.
78 I. Howard Marshall, *Kept by the Power of God* (Minneapolis, MN: Bethany House, 1969), 174-175.
79 Donald Barnhouse, *Messages to the Seven Churches* (Philadelphia, PA: Eternity Book Service, 1953), 38.

as opposed to the one who is not.[80]

Samuel Hoyt writes about the Judgment Seat of Christ. Concerning overcomers, He says, "Those who put believers in Christ into two different categories teach that believers who live victorious lives will reign with Christ during the Millennium."[81] But he explains, "the rest, who are carnal, non-victorious believers will fail the victory test at the Judgment Seat of Christ. As a result, these who fail to be victorious Christians will experience weeping, wailing, and gnashing of teeth in outer darkness."[82] He mentions, "for this writer is that the overcomers referred to in 1 John and the book of Revelation are all believers who make up the church of Jesus Christ."[83] George Zeller argues in support of all Christians being victorious and included as overcomers. He opposes the other view.[84] Conversely, Hoyt lists the names of those who teach only the victorious will be rewarded at the Judgment Seat and experience favored positions during the kingdom–millennium. Former Dallas Theological Seminary Professor Zane Hodge, Robert Govett, Robert Wilkins, Joseph Dillow, Tony Evans, and Charles Stanley are mentioned.[85] According to Hoyt, these divide the church into two categories. Both will experience two different destinies in the millennium. "The victorious overcomers rule and reign with Christ in the Millennial Kingdom while the barren or carnal believers suffer some measure of punishment or separation during the millennial reign of Christ."[86] Overcomers achieve their status by earning it.

Hoyt cites 1 John 5:4-5 as support for the view all believers are overcomers and therefore all will be rewarded during the millennium. John writes, "For whatsoever is born of God overcometh the world: and this is the victory that overcometh the world, even our faith. Who is he that overcometh the world, but he that believeth that Jesus is the Son of God?" (1 John 5:4-5). "Whoever believes" is in the present tense in both places (Rev. 2-3 and 1 John 5:4-5).[87] Hoyt interprets 1

---

80   Dillow, 479.
81   Samuel Hoyt, *The Judgment Seat of Christ* (Duluth, MN: Grace Gospel Press, 2011), 197.
82   Ibid.
83   Ibid., 204.
84   Ibid., 197.
85   Ibid., 198.
86   Ibid., 199.
87   Ibid., 200.

John 5:4-5 and Revelation 2 and 3, as being the same overcomers.[88] Although, he admits that some believers may be rewarded more than others.[89] But he rejects the idea that there will be two destinations for believers. One will be the Millennial Kingdom and the other outer darkness.[90]

According to Hoyt, being an overcomer is not earned; rather it is based on who dwells within the believer.[91] He cites Revelation 21:7 as a proof text. "He that overcometh shall inherit all things; and I will be his God, and he shall be my son" (Rev. 21:7). All believers are included in this passage (Rev. 21:3-5, 7-8). In these verses, the saved and the unsaved are mentioned–not two types of Christians. Hoyt argues that verse eight describes unsaved people rather than carnal and sinning believers. "But the fearful, and unbelieving, and the abominable, and murders, and whoremongers, and sorcerers, and idolaters, and all liars, shall have their part in the lake which burneth with fire and brimstone: which is the second death" (Rev. 21:8).

Dillow argues against this view that all believers are overcomers. "Inherit" is a key word (Rev. 21:7). In his comments on the passage in Revelation 21:7, he says, "The advocates of perseverance connect this inheritance with eternal life which comes to all who know Christ. However, consistent with its usage throughout the Bible the word "inherit" is once again a reward for faithful service (e.g., Col. 3:24)."[92] In Dillow's mind, all the saints will inhabit (residents) the New Jerusalem but only the overcomers will rule (rulers) there.[93] They will be blessed with special honors.

Three values of the overcomer are listed by Dillow that separate him from the carnal. First, there is a thirst. "I am Alpha and Omega … I will give to him that is athirst of the fountain of water of life freely" (Rev. 21:6). While eternal life is a free gift (Eph. 2:8-9), rewards will be earned. It will cost the believer a life of yieldedness and sacrifice. Not all Christians are willing to die to self and take up a cross to follow Jesus as a disciple. Some will choose to live for self (Matt. 10:38-39;

---

88 Hoyt, 200.
89 Ibid.
90 Ibid., 201.
91 Ibid., 200.
92 Dillow, 471.
93 Ibid.

Gal. 5:24; Rom. 13:14, 6:11; Gal. 2:20), rather than submitting to Jesus' Lordship (Col. 2:6). "As ye have received Christ Jesus as Lord, so walk ye in him" (Col. 2:6). This does not advocate perfection but it does distinguish those who are spirit-filled verses those who are carnal minded (Rom. 8:1-8; 13-14; Gal. 5:16-17).

Second, Dillow explains the term "son" used in Revelation 21:7. "He that overcometh … I will be his God, and he shall be my son." According to him "son" is not defined as regeneration but special honor.[94] The word indicates "sonship is (huioi, mature sons, not tekna, children) by a life of obedience. All Christians are children (Gk, tekna) but not all are obedient mature sons (Gk, huioi)." Dillow notes, Paul integrates "children" (tekna) with "sons" (huioi), but John does not.[95]

Third, after examining Revelation 21:6 and 7, Dillow says that John describes the destination of the unbelievers in Revelation 21:8. This is contradictory to what Hoyt mentions in his book. Dillow is not describing carnal Christians in Revelation 21:8, but rather unbelievers.

Dillow argues the passage in Revelation 22:14 is not for all believers but just for those who have overcome. "Blessed are they that do his commandments, that they may have right to the tree of life, and may enter in through the gates into the city" (Rev. 22:14). He carries the reader back to the origin of the tree of life in Genesis 3:22 and 24. Regeneration is free but access to the tree of life is not without cost according to him.[96] This is for those who have persevered. Special privileges are reserved for the overcomers. Donald Barnhouse writes,

> Some have said that eating from the tree of life was the equivalent of receiving eternal life, but this is most evidently a false interpretation. Eternal life is the prerequisite for membership in the true Church. Eating of the tree of life is a reward that shall be given to the overcomer in addition to his salvation … He receives over and above his entrance into eternal life, a place in the Heavens in the midst of the paradise of God.[97]

---

94   Dillow, 471.
95   Ibid., 472.
96   Ibid., 474.
97   Donald Barnhouse, *Revelation: An Expository Commentary* (Grand Rapids, MI: Zondervan, 1971), 43-44, quoted in Dillow, 474-475.

Dillow remarks that the "garments" mentioned in Revelation 22:14, are the righteous acts of the saints.[98]

Dillow, refuting the Reformer's doctrine writes, "The book of Revelation does not teach that all believers will rule over the millennial earth. Only the crowned and rewarded church in heaven rules (Rev. 4:10; 5:10) ... it is true all believers will in one sense 'reign forever and ever (Rev. 22:5)."[99] In summary, he teaches that all believers will enjoy fellowship with Christ in eternity but with varying degrees. He argues why would God warn Christians if all are overcomers?

Are all Christians overcomers because of their position in Christ? Is this judicial? Does this mean all Christians are overcomers practically? Paul wrote to the carnal Christians in Corinth (1 Cor. 3). Was Lot an overcomer?

While Dillow's purpose for writing his book was to explain the role of overcoming Christians in this life and how that will affect their role in the kingdom to come, he did acknowledge the nation of Israel's reign with Christ. He says,

> Often in the Old Testament, salvation has messianic overtones. It refers to the future regathering of the nation of Israel and their establishment as rulers in a universal kingdom under the kingship of David's greater Son. It is not surprising then to find that both *sozo* and *soteria* often have similar connotations in the New Testament: joint participation with Christ in the coming kingdom rule.[100]

He builds his case by integrating meanings of certain words: One word is "inherit" (Gk, kleronmeo) which means "to possess, to own. The lexicons define the word as to 'receive as one's own'[101] to acquire,

---

98   Dillow, 475.
99   Ibid., 478.
100   Ibid., 127.
101   G. Abbott-Smith, *A Manual Greek Lexicon of the New Testament* (Edinburgh: T&T Clark, 1937), 248, quoted in Dillow, 79-80.

obtain, come into possession of."[102] While he uses passages of Scripture in the gospels and Paul's writings relating to an inheritance, he seems to recognize the Jewish promises (technical interpretation), but he draws practical application to the church during the kingdom.[103] He quotes Robertson and Plummer, "To inherit the 'kingdom of God' is a Jewish thought, in allusion to the promises given to Abraham."[104] He explains, "Similarly, in the New Testament, inheriting the kingdom is conditioned upon spiritual obedience and not faith alone."[105] He concludes by saying, "All saints will enter the kingdom through faith alone (John 3), but only obedient saints who endure, who overcome, and perform works of righteousness (e.g. ministering to Christ's brethren) will inherit it, i.e., rule there."[106]

Dillow uses the word "partaker" (*metochos*) which means "partner or companion."[107] After citing a passage in Hebrews (3:14) as well as others, he connects the word with believers partaking in the kingdom. "For we are made partakers of Christ if we hold the beginning of our confidence to the end." He concludes, "The metochoi of King Jesus then are His co-heirs in the rulership of the messianic kingdom."[108]

In refuting Hoyt's critique of the phrase "weeping and gnashing of teeth" in relation to carnal believers during the kingdom, Dillow clarifies the phrase is mentioned seven times in the New Testament.[109] Jesus mentioned it three times describing the unregenerate (Matt. 13:42, 50; Luke 13:28). However, four times it is mentioned of the regenerate in the kingdom (Matt. 8:12; 22:13; 24:51; 25:30).[110] Dillow says, "It seems that these verses adequately explain the experience of profound regret for the unfaithful Christian which Matthew calls

---

102 William F. Arndt and F. Wilbur Gingrich, *A Greek-English Lexicon of the New Testament and Other Early Christian Literature* (Chicago, IL: University of Chicago Press, 1957), 436, quoted in Dillow, 79-80.
103 Dillow, 75-110.
104 Archibald Robertson and Alfred A. Plummer, *Critical and Exegetical Commentary on the First Epistle of St. Paul to the Corinthians*, 2nd Ed. The International Critical Commentary (Edinburgh: T&T Clark, 1914), 118, quoted in Dillow, 77.
105 Dillow, 77.
106 Ibid., 82.
107 Arndt and Gingrich, *A Greek–English Lexicon of the New Testament and Other Early Christian Literature*, 516, quoted in Dillow, 102.
108 Dillow, 105.
109 Ibid., 351.
110 Ibid.

'wailing and gnashing of teeth.'"[111] Blomberg argues against Dillow's interpretation. He explains,

> The picture of the slave caught beating his fellow servant does not portray Christians caught in sin and suddenly damned. Instead, it pictures people who delay coming to terms with God in Christ for too long, so that they suddenly find, whether due to his return or due to their own deaths, that it is too late to repent.[112]

J. Vernon McGee's conclusion is everybody needs to be ready for Christ's return. Both saved and lost will give an account. Technically, he says, "It has application to us, although the interpretation is specifically to folk living at the time of Christ's return."[113]

Commenting on Matthew 24:51, "weeping and gnashing of teeth," Toussaint writes, "Invariably throughout Matthew this phrase refers to the retribution of those who are judged before the millennial kingdom is established (Matt. 8:12; 13:42, 50; 22:13; 25:30).[114] Dillow summarizes Lang who writes, "Those Christians who fail to persevere to the end, who are carnal, will experience three negatives at the future judgment: (1) a stinging rebuke (Matt. 24:45-51), (2) exclusion from the wedding banquet (Matt. 22:1-14; 25:1-13), and (3) millennial disinheritance (Matt. 25:14-30)."[115] However, this interpretation can be problematic. Dillow argues that Matthew 24:45-51 refers to Christians.[116] The first problem is this would be in the context of the second coming of Christ when Christians have been raptured. Second, this would have been better interpreted as to the Jewish people not Christians. Third, this would have been during the tribulation.

The debate of what is meant by the term "overcomer" will continue. All will concur that Jesus overcame (John 16:33). Because of

---

111 Dillow, 351.
112 Blomberg, 368.
113 J. Vernon McGee, *Thru the Bible*. Vol. 4 (Nashville, TN: Thomas Nelson, 1983), 133.
114 Toussaint, 282.
115 G.H. Lang, *Pictures and Parables* (Miami Springs, FL: Conley and Schoettle, 1985), 308, quoted in Dillow, 353.
116 Dillow, 385.

that truth, all are overcomers (1 John 5:4-5). In a practical sense, each believer this side of the kingdom has choices every day whether he or she will overcome the flesh or surrender to the Spirit (Gal. 5:16-24; Rom. 8:13-14; 13:14; Gal. 2:20). There is always victory in Jesus (1 Cor. 15:57, 58). This writer is not sure of Dillow's view on the rapture.

The Church and the Kingdom – Judgment Seat "bema"

Proponents of the general judgment theory teach that there will be one final judgment. It will take place at the consummation of the world. However, the opponents of this general judgment theory point to the Judgment Seat of Christ as a separate judgment. This Judgment Seat of Christ will only be for believers according to them. Some Protestants as well as Roman Catholics embrace the general judgment view. Postmillennialists and amillennialists teach this perspective.[117] Does the Bible teach there is going to be a general judgment? Or does it teach there will be a sequence of judgments?

An opponent of the general judgment concept is Merrill Unger. He writes of the damage it has inflicted on the protestant confessions:

> The error of a general judgment of the pre-reformation Church as brought over into the Lutheran Reformation and into Reformed Theology and as embedded briefly but powerfully in the great Protestant creeds, such as the Augsburg Confession, the Thirty Nine Articles, and the Westminster Confession, is too well established and attested for many otherwise great theologians to see beyond the confusion to "what saith the Scriptures?"[118]

Hoyt names some proponents of the general judgment such as Charles Hodge (a Presbyterian postmillennialist), W.G.T. Shedd (a millennialist), Louis Berkhof (a Reformed amillennialist), and A.H.

---

117 Hoyt, 16.
118 Ibid., 19.

Strong (a Baptist postmillennialist).[119] But there are those who refute the general judgment theory such as Lewis Sperry Chafer. According to him, there will be five major judgments reserved for future times: (1) Church-age believer's judgment (1 Cor. 3:11-15; 2 Cor. 5:10), (2) The nation of Israel (Ezek. 20:33-38); Matt. 24:37-25:30), (3) The Gentile nations (Joel 3:2-16; Matt. 25:31-46), (4) The fallen angels (2 Pet. 2:4; Jude 1:6), and (5) The great white throne Jjdgment (Rev. 20:11-15).[120]

The improper method of interpretation leads to erroneous conclusions. John Walvoord explains the difference in the correct way opposed to the incorrect way.

> There is a growing realization in the theological world that the crux of the millennial issue is the question of the *method* of interpreting Scripture. Premillenarians follow the so-called 'grammatical–historical' literal interpretation while amillenarians use a spiritualizing method.[121]

He explains that in the third century the Alexandrian school of theology used the allegorical method of interpretation. Augustine set the example that many are modeling today which uses the spiritualized approach to interpret Bible Prophecy. Yet in the historical and doctrinal parts of the Bible, he taught the historical–grammatical literal method of interpretation. Augustine influenced many of the Protestant Reformers with his amillennialism teaching.[122]

Pentecost concurs with Walvoord. He writes,

> No question facing the student of Eschatology is more important than the question of the method to be employed in the interpretation of the prophetic Scripture. …The basic differences between the premillennial and

---

119 Hoyt, 21.
120 Lewis Chafer, *Systematic Theology*, vol. 4: Ecclesiology – Eschatology (Dallas, TX: Dallas Seminary Press, 1948), 404-412.
121 John Walvoord, *The Millennial Kingdom* (Grand Rapids, MI: Dunham Publishing Company, 1959), 59, quoted in Hoyt, 23.
122 Ibid., 60, quoted in Hoyt, 24.

amillennial schools and between the pretribulation and postribulation rapturists are hermeneutical, arising from the adoption of divergent and irreconcilable methods of interpretation.[123]

According to Hoyt, amillennialists use both the literal method and the spiritualizing method of interpreting Scripture. Utilizing the proper rules and guidelines from the beginning and practicing consistency throughout the task achieves the ultimate goal, which is to develop a correct understanding of the Bible. This is the purpose of this study namely, to discover God's plan for the church and His kingdom.

Does Paul teach there is going to be a judgment for Christians? A careful examination of Scripture will reveal that there will be more than the general judgment. The substantial evidence points to a resurrection when all believers will appear before the Judgment Seat of Christ. Other judgments will follow in the future.

According to Hoyt, the word "judgment seat" is the translation of the Greek word *bema*, which Paul's culture understood.[124] The word "*bema* comes from the Greek verb *baino*, which means to go up or ascend."[125] It pictures a platform with steps. However, it is used in the Septuagint (derived from the Old Testament) twice and describes a pulpit (Neh. 8:4; Deut. 2:5).[126] According to Francis Brown, S.R. Driver, and Charles A. Briggs, "the word bema is used to translate the Hebrew word *migdal* which means an elevated stage or pulpit of wood."[127]

Bema is used twelve times in the New Testament. Two references are used in an eschatological way (2 Cor. 5:10; Rom. 14:10). The other ten usages of *bema* are in relation to historical events. Hoyt notes that even though *bema* is used with different terms in 2 Corinthians 5:10 and Romans 14:10, there is no contradiction. He says,

---

123   Pentecost, *Things to Come*, 1.
124   Hoyt, 33.
125   G. Abbott Smith, *A Manual Greek Lexicon of the New Testament*, 3rd Ed. (Edinburgh: T&T Clark, 1937), 80, quoted in Hoyt, 32.
126   Hoyt, 34.
127   Francis Brown, S.R. Driver, and Charles A Briggs, eds., *The Hebrew and English Lexicon of the Old Testament with an Appendix Containing the Biblical Aramaic* (Oxford: Clarendon Press, 1907), 153-154, quoted in Hoyt, 34.

> W. Robert Cook suggests an explanation for the difference in these references: 'In 2 Corinthians 5:10 this judgment is called the "judgment-seat of Christ" and thus the person of the one before whom we will stand is emphasized, but in Romans 14:10, where the same judgment is in view, it is called the "judgment-seat of God" (A.S.V.) for there the emphasis is upon deity of the one before whom we will stand.'[128]

Both verses refer to the same event.

Hoyt builds his case of the "judgment seat" (*bema*) of Christ being only for Christians. He points out the error of the general judgment theory by doing an exegetical analysis of 2 Corinthians 5:10 and 1 Corinthians 3:11-16. This all fits into God's plan for the church in relation to the kingdom. However, some (general judgment theory–one judgment) interpret that the Judgment Seat of Christ determines who goes to heaven and who does not. Louis Berkhof writes, "The last judgment determines, and therefore naturally leads on to, the final state of those who appear before the Judgment Seat. Their final state is either one of everlasting misery or one of eternal blessedness."[129] An improper method of interpretation of Scripture leads to misunderstanding of other Scripture.

If the Judgment Seat (*bema*) of Christ is going to affect the church and fulfill God's plan just before the kingdom, several questions become pertinent. How long will the Judgment Seat of Christ last and where will it take place? How will a believer (the church) be judged? Will there be losses and gains? What will its purpose be?

In his second epistle to the church of Corinth, Paul wrote, "For we must all appear before the Judgment Seat of Christ; that every one may receive the things *done* in *his* body, according to that he hath done, whether *it be* good or bad" (2 Cor. 5:10). The bema judgment will take place after the rapture of the Church (1 Cor. 3:11-14; 2 Tim. 4:7-8; 1 Cor. 9:24-27; Dan. 12:3; 1 Pet. 5:4; James 1:12; 1 Thess. 2:19).

---

128   William Robert Cook, "The Judgment Seat of Christ as Related to the Believer" (Paper presented to the Professor of Systematic Theology, Dallas Theological Seminary, May 1953), 2-3, quoted in Hoyt, 35.

129   L. Berkhof, *Systematic Theology*, 4th Ed. (Grand Rapids, MI: William B. Eerdmans Publishing, 1941), 735, quoted in Hoyt, 75.

Another passage of Scripture that describes this event is found in 1 Corinthians 3:13. "Every man's work shall be made manifest: for the day shall declare it, because it shall be revealed by fire: and the fire shall try every man's work of what sort it is." Hoyt suggests, "The day" follows the verb *apokalyptetai* which reveals with fire the substance.[130] The timing of this event is connected with 1 Corinthians 4:5 which reads, "Therefore judge nothing before the time, until the Lord come, who will bring to light the hidden things of darkness, and will make manifest the counsels of the hearts: and then shall every man have praise of God." Hoyt concludes, "Clearly, then, the *bema* does not occur until Christ returns for His church."[131]

How long will this Judgment Seat last? According to George Ladd, seven years is not enough time. He writes, "If a period of time intervene for this judgment to take place will seven years be enough? It is estimated that there are two hundred million living Christians. In seven years, there are just over two hundred million seconds … If an interval of time is needed, then far more than seven years will be required."[132] Both Haldeman and M.R. DeHaan believe that the Judgment Seat of Christ could last the entire seven years.[133] However, Lehman Strauss and Leon Wood argue against Ladd's view. Strauss writes, "It is possible that this judgment of the saints will be instantaneous, and that each Christian will rise into the air to enter at once into his proper place and appointed rewarding."[134] This author concludes that if God can make the universe in just six literal days, then He will not have a problem judging at the Judgment Seat of Christ.

Where will this judgment take place? There remains a debate on this subject. Some conclude it will take place in the air. James M. Gray, speaking on meeting Christ in the air, explains, "It serves as the location of the judgment and for the adjudication of our rewards

---

130   Hoyt, 48.
131   Ibid.
132   George Eldon Ladd, *The Blessed Hope* (Grand Rapids, MI: Eerdmans Pub., 1956), 103.
133   Hoyt, 52.
134   Lehman Strauss, *We Live Forever: A Study of Life After Death* (New York, NY: Loizeaux Brothers, 1947), 73, quoted in Samuel Hoyt, *The Judgment Seat of Christ*, 51.

of our places in the coming kingdom."[135] Others, such as E. Schuyler English, teach the Judgment Seat will be in heaven.[136] Chafer concurs the Judgment Seat of Christ will be in heaven.[137]

Paul writes in 2 Corinthians 5:10, "For we must all appear before the Judgment Seat of Christ." Hoyt explains the word "before" is the Greek *emprosthen*.[138] It means "in that local region which is in front of a person or a thing."[139] This seems to be a reference to the saints (church) appearing before the throne of God (Rev. 4:2, 10).

Who will participate at the *bema*? The words "all appear before the Judgment Seat of Christ" reveal another insight. "All" is the word [pantes].[140] According to Hoyt, this means the totality of the Christian world.[141] No Christian will be exempt. W.E. Vines writes, "In the plural it [pas] signifies the totality of the persons or things referred to."[142] This should motivate believers to be faithful to God. The word "appear" is the Greek word *phaneroo*.[143] According to Unger, "The word is forceful–*phanerootheenai* [sic], meaning to be made manifest, be revealed in true character, be made plain or evident. The very character of each Christian will thus be laid bare. His inmost motives and purposes will be ascertained."[144] Daily examination of prayer and Bible study by every believer will help purify one's motives.

Will each believer stand before the Judgment Seat of Christ individually? "For we must all appear before the Judgment Seat of Christ." The Greek word *hekastos* "each" and "every" demonstrates this judg-

---

135 James M. Gray, "Christ the Executor of All Future Judgments in Christ in Glory" (Addresses delivered at the New York Prophetic Conference, Carnegie Hall, November 25-28, 1918), in *Our Hope*, Arno C. Gaebelein, ed. (New York: Publication Office, n.d.), 201-202, quoted in Hoyt, 55.

136 Hoyt, 55.

137 Ibid., 56.

138 Ibid, 55.

139 C.L. Wilibad Grimm, *Thayer's Greek-English Lexicon of the New Testament* (Grand Rapids, MI: Zondervan, 1962), 208, quoted in Hoyt, 55.

140 Hoyt, 60.

141 Ibid., 60.

142 W.E. Vines, *Vines Expository Dictionary of New Testament Words with their Precise Meanings for English Readers* (Westwood, NJ: Fleming H. Revel Company, 1940), 46, quoted in Hoyt, 60.

143 Hoyt, 97.

144 Merill F. Unger, "The Doctrine of the Believer's Judgment," in *Our Hope*, January 1952, 433, quoted in Hoyt 97.

ment will be an individual person, one at a time. Vines explains that this word "is used of any number separately."[145] Living righteously now will pay eternal dividends later.

What will be given to the church (believers) at the Judgment Seat (*bema*) of Christ before the kingdom period? Crowns will be given: the watchers (2 Tim. 4:7-8), runners (1 Cor. 9:24-27), soul winners (1 Thess. 2:19), faithful shepherd (1 Pet 5:4), and the crown of life (James 1:12). A believer who is making a difference in this life will be rewarded in the life to come. Motives will be tested. Some Christians will suffer loss although they will be saved (1 Cor. 3:11-14). Ultimately, rewards in the form of crowns will be cast before the throne of Jesus (Rev. 4:10-11). The Judgment Seat of Christ "bema" is not to be confused with the Great White Throne Judgment (Rev. 20:11-15) where only the lost will be judged and sentenced to the lake of fire. Only believers will be at the "bema," which will follow the rapture.

In the context of the Judgment Seat (bema) of Christ, what did Paul mean by receiving "whether good or bad"? (2 Cor. 5:10). Hoyt describes the meaning of both words *agathos* or *phaulos*, good or bad.[146] The word "bad" is not the usual word used which means corrupt or evil.[147] Richard Trench explains, "[It is] evil under another aspect, not so much that either of active or passive malignity, but that rather of its good-for-nothingness ... the notion of worthlessness is the central notion of *phaulos* (brackets and italics added)."[148] Arndt and Gingrich define the word bad, *phaulos* as "worthless, bad, evil, base."[149] Pentecost gives an excellent illustration to clarify the meaning of the word. He writes,

> What the apostle is saying here is that everyone is going to be examined to see whether that which he

---

145   W.E. Vines, *Vines Expository Dictionary of the New Testament with their Precise Meanings for English Readers* (Westwood, NJ: Fleming H. Revel Company, 1940), 9, quoted in Hoyt, 61.
146   Hoyt, 99.
147   Ibid.
148   Richard Chenevix Trench, *Synonyms of the New Testament* (Marshallton, DE: National Foundation for Christian Education, n.d.), 296-297, quoted in Hoyt, 99.
149   William F. Arndt and F. Wilbur Gingrich, *A Greek-English Lexicon of the New Testament and Other Early Christian Literature* (Chicago, IL: University of Chicago Press, 1979), 862, quoted in Hoyt, 99.

> has done is acceptable or unacceptable, whether it is suited to be designated use or is unsuited to a designated use … If you try to convert a pair of pliers into a hammer, you will have nothing but a bent nail … The pliers are perfectly good but unacceptable as a substitute hammer, The apostle is not speaking of that which is morally good as opposed to morally bad, but that which is usable or useful as opposed to that which is useless.[150]

At the Judgment Seat of Christ, the "bad" does not mean moral evil or wickedness. Rather, it means useless. Therefore, a believer will be judged to see if he or she is useful or not.

Will there be degrees for rewards for believers? Grudem writes, "Scripture also teaches that there will be degrees of rewards for believers."[151] There are two different foundations a believer can build upon, according to Paul. He writes in his letter to the Corinthians,

> For other foundation can no man lay than that is laid, which is Christ Jesus. Now if any man build upon this foundation gold, silver, precious stones, wood hay, stubble; Every man's work shall be made manifest: for the day shall declare, because it shall be revealed by fire; and the fire shall try every man's work of what sort it is. If any man's work abide which he hath built thereupon, he shall receive reward. If any man's work shall be burned, he shall suffer loss: but he himself shall be saved; yet so as by fire (1 Cor. 3:11-15).

This passage does not teach a loss of salvation but rather a loss of rewards. The term "suffer loss" is translated *zemioo* and it is in the passive form and means to forfeiture or suffer loss.[152] It does mean

---

150 Dwight J. Pentecost, *Prophecy for Today: An Exposition of Major Themes on Prophecy* (Grand Rapids, MI: Zondervan Publishing House, 1961), 154-155, quoted in Hoyt, 100.
151 Grudem, 1144.
152 Hoyt, 136.

to punish. Hoyt refutes Arndt and Gingrich's definition to punish.[153] Hoyt quotes Vines who says, "the passive voice means to suffer loss or to forfeit."[154] Robertson and Plummer concur the word means to forfeit.[155] Accountability is going to take place at the Judgment Seat of Christ. Each believer will either reap or forfeit rewards.

From this study of the Judgment Seat (*bema*) of Christ, several conclusions are drawn. God is not building His kingdom now through the church. Rather, He is training His church to overcome and preparing His church to participate in His kingdom when He inaugurates it. The church is getting ready for Jesus to come in the rapture. After the rapture, the church will appear before the Judgment Seat of Christ, and finally God's kingdom will come.

Questions for Review and Discussion

1. Discuss the meaning of Matthew 16:18, where Jesus tells Peter He will build His church.

2. List some passages of Scripture in the epistles of Paul that relate to the kingdom of God.

3. Explain the meaning of these passages in relation to the kingdom of God in the future or present.

4. Examine 1 Corinthians 15:20-24, and be ready to expound its meaning as it relates to the resurrection and the kingdom.

5. List the promises Jesus made to the churches in Revelation 2 and 3, preparing them for the kingdom to come.

---

153   William F. Arndt and F. Wilbur Gingrich, *A Greek-English Lexicon of the New Testament and Other Early Christian Literature* (Chicago, IL: University of Chicago Press, 1979), 339, quoted in Hoyt, 136.

154   W.E. Vines, *Vines Expository Dictionary of New Testament Words with their Precise Meanings for English Readers* (Westwood, NJ: Fleming H. Revel Company, 1940), 121, quoted in Hoyt, 136.

155   Archibald Robertson and Alfred A. Plummer, *A Critical and Exegetical Commentary on the First Epistle of Paul to the Corinthians*, 2nd Ed., The International Critical Commentary (Edinburgh: T&T Clark, 1941), 65, quoted in Hoyt 137.

6. Discuss the "Judgment Seat of Christ" (2 Cor. 5:10; Rom. 14:10; 1 Cor. 3:11-15)?
7. Explain the rewards (crowns) for believers and what is meant by losses?

Chapter Five

The King's Inauguration of the Kingdom (Rev. 19-20, Ezek. 40-48)

When is God's kingdom going to be on the earth? Are there indicators that His kingdom has come? How will the church participate in the kingdom? How long will the kingdom last? What is God's purpose for establishing His kingdom? This chapter is going to discuss the events prior to the inauguration of the kingdom and the description of the kingdom.

From Chapter 6 of the book of Revelation, progressing all the way to Chapter 19 of this apocalyptic literature, God's wrath and judgment will be released from heaven in the form of seven seals, trumpets, and vials. This is described as the tribulation period. The last three years of the seven years of tribulation (Dan. 9:27) will be the great tribulation (Rev. 12-19). All of this will bring about the fulfillment of God's purpose for the preservation of the Jewish people (Rev. 7, 14), the times of the Gentiles (Luke 21:24-28), the overthrow of Satan (Rev. 20:10), and the preparation of the earth and its dwellers for His kingdom to be established (Rev. 20).

These unparalleled events will lead up to the second coming of Christ after the tribulation. Before that event, the bloody battle called Armageddon will take place (Rev. 19:11-16; Zech. 14:1-4; Rev. 14:19-20). All the armies of the world, including the Antichrist (Zech. 14:2-3), will fight against the Lord only to be destroyed (Rev. 19:16).

The church reappears from being in heaven with Christ to join Him during the millennial kingdom. "And the armies which were in heaven followed him upon white horses, clothed in fine linen, white and clean" (Rev. 19:14). Then Jesus ushers in His kingdom (Rev. 20).

However, another prophetic passage to consider in the context of Christ's second coming and before His kingdom is found in Matthew 24 and 25. Jesus is responding to His disciples concerning the end times. The best interpretation from the text reveals this will be the second coming of Jesus in glory and power, not the rapture (Matt. 24:15; 24:27; 24:29; 24:36). There will be signs during the tribulation (Matt. 24:4-30; Luke 21:24-28), but no one knows the hour when He shall return (Matt. 24:36). The rapture passages are located in the following Scriptures: 1 Thess. 4:16-17; 1 Cor. 15:51-58; John 14:1-3; and Rev. 4:2.

Writing on Matthew 25, Toussaint says, "Matthew introduces the parable with his characteristic adverb 'then' (*tote*)."[1] This is the parable of the ten virgins. "Then shall the kingdom of heaven be likened unto ten virgins, which took their lamps, and went forth to meet the bridegroom" (Matt. 25:1). There is some debate on the correct interpretation of this passage. Toussaint notes that some teach that this is the church at the coming of Jesus.[2] He writes, "The premillenarians who hold this view contend that *tote* refers to Matthew 24:45-51 which is said to deal with the church."[3] Their argument is that the tribulation is too long to wait for His return. However, Toussaint puts that argument to rest when he writes, "This parable as well as the next one deals with the Jews in the tribulation period."[4] His evaluation is based on the context of Matthew 24:3, 8, 14, 15, 27, 30, 31, 33, 42, 47, and 51. The church will be absent from the earth during the tribulation. He argues, "The adverb 'then' (*tote*) of Matthew 25:1 connects this passage to Matthew 24:51."[5]

During the tribulation leading up to the second coming and the millennium, the Antichrist will emerge. The work of the Antichrist described as the "abomination of desolation" (Matt. 24:15; Dan. 9:27;

---

1 Toussaint, 283.
2 Ibid.
3 Ibid.
4 Ibid.
5 Ibid.

2 Thess. 2:4; Rev. 13) was partially fulfilled with Antiochus Epiphanes (167 B.C.) but will be completely fulfilled when the man of sin sits in the temple and is worshipped (Dan. 9:27; 2 Thess. 2:3-4; Matt. 24:15). At the conclusion of the tribulation, Christ will return and set up his kingdom (Rev. 19:11-14; Zech. 14:1-4). Following the battle of Armageddon (Rev. 14, 19; Dan. 11; Zech. 14), Jesus will sit on His throne and fulfill the Abrahamic, Davidic, Land, and New Covenant (Gen. 12:2; Sam. 7; Deut. 30; Jer. 31; Rev. 20). The Old Testament writers saw and wrote concerning the day of the Lord (Joel 2; Zech. 14), which literally will be fulfilled when Jesus comes again and sets up his millennial kingdom. DeYoung teaches that the day of the Lord has a general meaning (1,007 years) as well as a specific meaning (when Jesus sets his feet on the Mt. of Olives, Zech. 14:1-4).

Other events are mentioned in the Bible that will factor into the scenario prior to the kingdom. Daniel was given prophetic revelation. King Nebuchadnezzar was puzzled, but Daniel was prayerful. Both the rising of the Antichrist–as the "little horn" (Dan. 7:8, 25) and the "Times of the Gentiles" was revealed. Four world empires were seen (not including the Antichrist world power–Revived Roman Empire). These four were Babylon, Mede Persian, Grecian, and Roman. Jesus used the phrase the "Times of the Gentiles" in Luke 21:24. This phrase describes the time when Gentiles rule over the Jews and Jerusalem, which will last until the second coming of Christ (Rev. 19:11, 20-22).

In the same vision was the coming of the final world empire. Many Bible prophecy teachers including DeYoung believe this final world empire to be the Revived Roman Empire (Rev. 17), at least the infrastructure. Several reasons have been mentioned, both historically and biblically. Historically, the Old Roman Empire went inoperative in 476 A.D., according to DeYoung (Dan. 7:7). Furthermore, this empire has never been defeated. Biblically, Daniel's prophecy stated that the fourth world kingdom would "devour the whole earth" (Dan. 7:23). The little horn comes out of the fourth beast—a Gentile power. This prophecy is yet to be fulfilled. The Roman Empire did not devour the whole world.

In relation to the kingdom, Daniel had a vision of the "ancient of days" handing the kingdom over to the "Son of man" (Dan. 7:13-14). "And there was given unto him dominion, and glory, and a kingdom, that all people, nations, and languages, should serve him: his dominion is an everlasting dominion, which shall not pass away, and his kingdom *that* which shall not be destroyed." Walvoord concurred with other conservative scholars that this was to be interpreted as God the Father giving the kingdom to Jesus.[6]

While Jesus will reign for one thousand years during this kingdom period, as mentioned in this research, some scholars, such as Vlach, interpret 1 Corinthians 15:24 to mean that Jesus will hand back over the kingdom to the Father for eternity future.[7]

Some of Daniel's prophecy concerning the future for the Jewish people has already been fulfilled (Dan. 9:24-27), but some remains unfulfilled. The historical account of the crucifixion of the messiah was fulfilled (Dan. 9.26, the phrase "cut off"). The seven years (one week) foreshadowed in Daniel 9:27 has not happened, but will be fulfilled as the duration of the tribulation (Dan. 9:27; 2 Thess. 2:3-4; Rev. 6-18). This will happen just before the Messiah's kingdom is established on earth (Rev. 20).

Furthermore, in the kingdom, the Lord will finally give the land that He promised to Israel. DeYoung wrote in his daily devotional,

> God will be giving the Jews ten times what they have today. The actual borders start near the Nile River in Egypt extending north to the Euphrates River, taking in half of Egypt, all of Israel, Lebanon, Syria and Jordan. The borders go south along the Euphrates to the Persian Gulf, which will take in half of Iraq and three quarters of Saudi Arabia. All of this real estate is promised to the Jewish people. Ezekiel starts to reveal only a portion of all that God will give the Jews.[8]

God is going to keep His covenant with His people (Gen. 12-15; Deut. 30). Likewise, He is going to keep His promise to the church (1 Thess. 4:13-18).

---

6 John Walvoord, *Daniel* (Chicago, IL: Moody Press, 1971), 166-167.
7 Vlach, 443-445.
8 Jimmy DeYoung, "Prophetic Prospective Daily Devotional: Ezekiel 48:1," entry posted January 18, 2018, http://devotional.prophecytoday.com/search?q=Ezekiel+48 (accessed August 20, 2018).

Millennium – 1000 years

According to Grudem, "the word *millennium* means 'one thousand years' (from Latin. *millennium*, thousand years)."[9] The word *millennium* comes from the passage of Scripture in Revelation 20:4-5. "And they lived and reigned with Christ a thousand years." Walvoord writes from a premillennial perspective and says, "The six mentions of a 'thousand years' in the passage are sufficient to establish the doctrine as scriptural."[10] Vlach quotes Robert Mounce who explains, "It should be noted that the recurring 'and I saw' of 19:11, 17, 19; 20:1, 4, 12; and 21:1, appears to establish a sequence of visions which carries through from the appearance of the Rider on the white horse (Rev. 19:11) to the establishment of the new heaven and new earth (21:1ff)."[11] Another writer shares his insight. Waymeyer says, "There is nothing in Revelation 20:1 that indicates a chronological break between the two chapters...."[12] A chronological order of sequence of events sets the precedence for the kingdom to be established.

Six of the eight visions start with "I saw" (Rev. 19:11- 21:8). According to Vlach, two of these visions are misinterpreted, being Revelation 20:1-3 and 4-7.[13] Both amillennialists and postmillennialists place these sections of Scripture between the two comings of Jesus.[14] Blaising, Mounce, and Blomberg disagree. They stand against those views. All concur that these sequences of visions found in Revelation 20:1-4 have nothing to do with Jesus coming again. Rather, this is a description of the resurrection of those (saints, not the church) who are martyred during the tribulation.

---

9   Grudem, 1109.
10   John Walvoord, *The Revelation of Jesus Christ* (Chicago, IL: Moody Press, 1966), 285.
11   Robert Mounce, *The Book of Revelation*, New International Commentary on the New Testament (Grand Rapids, MI: Eerdmans, 1977), 352, quoted in Vlach, 491.
12   Matthew Waymeyer, "What about Revelation 20?" in *Christ's Prophetic Plans: a Futuristic Premillennial Primer*, ed. John MacArthur and Richard Mayhue (Chicago, IL: Moody Press, 2012), 136.
13   Vlach, 492.
14   Ibid.

Millennium (Kingdom) Theological Views

There are three main views on the doctrine of the "millennium." This eschatological teaching is divided into three categories: The premillennial, amillennial, and postmillennial views. Only one of these three views is correct. Which one does the Bible describe?

The premillennial perspective approaches the one-thousand-year period as a literal time. This is based on the twentieth chapter of the book of Revelation. This view also incorporates the Old Testament passages associated with the millennium.

The postmillennial teaching has its meaning based on reformed theology. Israel is replaced by the church. There were some prominent proponents who supported this view. Kenneth Gentry mentions some of the early church fathers who were postmillennialists: Origen (A.D. 185-253), Eusebius (A.D. 260-340), Athanasius (A.D. 296-372), and Augustine (A.D. 354 -430).[15]

Writers such as Johnathan Edwards, William Carey, Robert Haldane, Henry Morris III, Augustus Strong, H.G. Moule, and Kenneth Gentry embraced this view.[16] Other terms that describe this view are Dominionism Theology and Christian Reconstructionism. Postmillennialism teaching has been discovered not only in early church writings but also with modern day writers. This view escalated under the Puritans and Reformers, both in England and America, during the seventeenth and nineteenth century.[17] John Calvin was one who popularized postmillennialism.

> Another feature of theonomic postmillennialism (though not essential to it) is its preterist approach to a number of great judgment passages in the New Testament. The preterist (Latin: 'gone by') approach to certain prophecies holds that the Great Tribulation (Matt. 24:21) occurred in the generation living when Christ spoke (Matt. 24:34).[18]

---

15 Gundry and Bock, *Three Views on the Millennial and Beyond*, 15-16.
16 Ibid., 18.
17 Ibid., 16.
18 Ibid., 21.

A preterist interprets the prophetic Scriptures in Revelation as already fulfilled. This would be opposite of those who view certain apocalyptic Scripture as futuristic.

Postmillennialism teaches that the Great Commission in this world will result in a largely Christian culture. The world will become more righteous. The use of the parables of the mustard seed and leaven teach that the kingdom of God will gradually grow. While refuting that view, some point to the words of Jesus, which said that wide and broad was the gate that led to destruction, and straight and narrow was the gate that led to everlasting life. According to Jesus, many would choose the wide and broad way, but only a few would choose the right way (Matt. 7:13-14).

The postmillennial view teaches the covenants God made with Abraham and the Jews are fulfilled in the church. Several chapters in the Psalms are used to justify this perspective (Psalm 2, 22, 67, 72, 110). Presently, Christ is ruling over His theocratic kingdom from heaven. This view teaches that His kingdom does not wait for His visible return or reign but rather He is ruling right now. Jesus has received His kingly authority (Acts 2:30-31; Matt. 28:18-20). Their interpretation of Revelation 20 is symbolic instead of literal. Furthermore, the first resurrection is a spiritual one not a literal one. Jesus has already defeated the devil so therefore He is reigning presently. According to this view, when He returns the end of the world will happen.

1. In response to the postmillennial view, a closer examination reveals it leaves off "the day of the Lord," which is a key phrase in God's overall scheme of things.
2. The last two thousand years needs an historical explanation if Jesus has been ruling and reigning on earth.
3. Psalm 2, Isaiah 2, Matthew 13 and 28, and 1 Cor. 15:20-28, were not interpreted from a literal, grammatical, historical perspective.

Dwight Pentecost summarized the postmillenarian features.

> Postmillennialism is based on the figurative interpreta-

tion of prophecy which permits wide freedom in finding the meaning of difficult passages–a latitude which is reflected in the lack of uniformity in postmillennial exegesis. The prophecies of the Old Testament relative to a righteous kingdom on earth are to be fulfilled in the kingdom of God in the interadvent period. The kingdom is spiritual and unseen rather than material and political....The throne which Christ is predicted to occupy is the Father's throne in heaven....There is no hope of the Lord's return in the foreseeable future, certainly not in this generation.[19]

The amillennial view teaches that the present age is now in the millennial. This perspective claims that there is only one passage of Scripture that refers to the millennial and it is found in Revelation 20. Several comments can be made. Augustine was a proponent of amillennialism. According to this view, Christ is the true Israel. The land of Canaan possession was fulfilled in Christ. Revelation 14:1, Micah 4:1-3, and Isaiah 2:2-4 are not future, but are interpreted as happening now. The Davidic covenant is already fulfilled. Jesus is the temple. Therefore, there will be no future temple. The amillennial doctrine suggests that Jesus fulfills God's promises to Israel (Rom. 11:7; Jer. 31:33). According to this teaching, the New Testament rules out a future millennial kingdom, because when Christ comes again everything will happen at once–resurrection of believers (1 Cor. 15:51) and unbelievers, judgment for all, the new heaven and the new earth, and the final state of the redeemed. Robert Strimple interprets 2 Peter 3:10-14 as the coming of Christ during the day of the Lord when the earth is destroyed, not leaving any time for the thousand-year reign.[20] This view is problematic.

Stanley Grenz, an amillennialist, writes referring to Romans 9-11, and states that God did not intend a thousand-year kingdom on earth in order to fulfill His promise to Israel. The thought is that the fullness of both the Jews and Gentiles will happen with no need for a future one thousand years. He says that this hope for Israel does not

---

19   Pentecost, *Things to Come*, 386.
20   Gundry and Bock, *Three Views on the Millennial and Beyond*, 151.

"require an earthly millennial reign of Christ, for the conversion of Israel could easily prepare for the inauguration of the eternal state as for an earthly golden age."[21] Grenz neglects to identify any reference to the Jews' possession of the land or the millennial kingdom in which Christ will reign from His throne in Jerusalem.

In response to the amillennial view, Blaising points out that Paul uses the term Israel in Romans 9-11, as the nation as a whole. "The nation is composed of two parts, the elect remnant and the rest, who are hardened, who have stumbled."[22] He explains, "Paul moves from the idea of the present existence of a remnant of faith to the future salvation of all Israel in accordance with covenant promise…. The future tense in 'will be saved' points to this salvation as a future reality."[23] He concludes, "The term *Israel* to refer to ethnic Jews, a believing remnant of which anticipates the salvation of the nation as a whole at the return of Christ."[24]

Vlach proposes an important question. "Is Israel's repentance a precondition for the establishment of the Messianic Kingdom?"[25] He answers that question in the affirmative and gives references (Jer. 3:11-18; Hos. 5:13-6:3; Zech. 12:1-10). Arnold Fruchtenbaum agrees as he writes, "confession of Israel's national sin is a major precondition that must be met before Christ will return to establish the Messianic Kingdom."[26] Grudem is an opponent of this view because he views the church as the "new Israel."[27] He avoids commenting on Romans 11:25-26. Rather, he says, "Even on the nondispensational view, a person may hold that there will be a future large-scale conversion of the Jewish believers becoming part of the true church of God—they will be 'grafted back into their own olive tree' (Rom. 11:24)."[28] Regardless of what others say, God is going to fulfill His promises to His people. This will include both Israel and the church. During the millennium kingdom, both will come to fruition.

---

21   Gundry and Bock, *Three Views on the Millenial and Beyond*, 113.
22   Ibid., 147.
23   Ibid., 148.
24   Ibid.
25   Vlach, 100.
26   Arnold Fruchtenbaum, *Israelology: The Missing Link in Systematic Theology* (Tustin, CA: Ariel Ministries Press, 1989), 781, 784.
27   Grudem, 861.
28   Ibid.

Grudem lets the reader know his position, "The position advocated in this book is historic premillennialism."[29] He notes that the word "pre" means "before." The "premillennial" view is that Jesus will come back before the millennium. Another word used for premillennialism is *"chiliasm."* The Greek word is "chilioi" which means a thousand.[30] It was used mostly in older literature according to Grudem. He explains the difference in Classic or (Historic) Premillennialism and Pretribulation (Dispensational) Premillennialism. "According to this viewpoint, the present church age will continue until, as it nears the end, a time of great tribulation and suffering comes upon the earth."[31] In other words, the church goes through the tribulation. He clarifies his position, "After that time of tribulation at the end of the church age, Christ will return to the earth to establish a millennial kingdom."[32] Grudem's theological persuasion teaches the post tribulation rapture. As already noted earlier, this writer's conviction is directed toward the pre-tribulation (rapture) view. However, as one can conclude, that is why Grudem and others teach the "kingdom now" theology, rather than the "church now" and the "kingdom later." This view leaves out solid evidence from other verses of Scripture.

However, Grudem is correct in describing the kingdom period. "Christ will be physically present on the earth in his resurrected body, and will reign over the entire earth."[33] According to him, many, but not all, unbelievers on earth will trust in Jesus and be saved.[34] In describing the kingdom (millennial) period, Grudem says,

> Many premillennialists hold that the earth will be renewed and we will in fact see the new heavens and new earth at this time (but not essential to premillennialism to hold to this, for one could be a premillennialist and hold that the new heavens and the new earth will not occur until after the final judgment).[35]

---

29   Grudem, 1127.
30   Ibid.
31   Ibid., 1112.
32   Ibid.
33   Ibid.
34   Ibid.
35   Ibid.

The timing of the new heaven and new earth is viewed differently. Some teach it will happen during the millennium. Others teach that it will happen immediately at the conclusion of the millennium.

Craig Blaising writes about another writer who taught from the Historic Premillennial perspective, George Ladd. Blaising mentions that in the mid-twentieth century some premillennialists such as Ladd "sought to distinguish themselves from classical dispensationalism by using the label historic premillennialism."[36] He uses another term "holistic premillennialism" that fit Ladd as well. According to Blaising, Ladd's historic premillennialism "functioned primarily as a rallying point in the twentieth century for nondispensationalists."[37] Speaking of Ladd, Feinberg, says, "Ladd takes a safe position on Revelation 20:1 in his statement: 'It is an open question as to whether the binding of Satan in Revelation 20 is the same as that in Matthew 12 [vv. 28, 29] or is an eschatological event.'"[38] Ryrie says about Ladd.

> In representing the covenant premillennial viewpoint, Ladd has been criticized ... by non dispensationalist ... that the doctrine of the millennium is not sufficiently integrated into the author's overall view of the kingdom. If there are no Old Testament prophecies which demand a literal, earthly fulfillment, then the purpose of the millennium becomes partially obscure.[39]

Ladd believes that there is only one place in the Bible that supports the millennial doctrine (Rev. 20:1-10). However, this opinion is disputed with verifiable evidence.

Ladd uses the symbolic method of interpretation throughout the book of Revelation. Therefore, he concludes the opposite of the literal understanding of the text. In response to his conclusion, there are certain guidelines for interpreting apocalyptic literature as dis-

---

36   George Ladd, *Crucial Questions About the Kingdom* (Grand Rapids, MI: Eerdmans, 1952), no page no., quoted in Gundry, *Three Views on the Millennial and Beyond*, 186-187.
37   Gundry and Bock, *Three Views on the Millennial and Beyond*, 189.
38   George Ladd, *A Commentary on the Revelation of John* (Grand Rapids, MI: Eerdmans, 1972), 260, quoted in Charles L. Feinberg, *Millennialism* (Winona Lake, IN: BMH Books, 1985), 331.
39   Ryrie, *Dispensationalism*, 173-174.

cussed already in this document. Furthermore, he along with others, rejects that there are any Old Testament references to the millennial. Their view is the kingdom of God has already come when Jesus was on earth. However, they (amillennialists) also confuse the battle of Armageddon (Rev. 16:14; 19:19) with the battle of Gog and Magog (Rev. 20:8). A response to the amillennial view is as follows. The Old Testament only uses a few verses to introduce the coming of the Messiah. Secondly, there are several Old and New Testament Scriptures besides Revelation 20 that refer to the millennial (Isa. 11:2-5; 65:20; Zech. 14:6-21; Rev. 2:27; 12:5; 19:15).

Blaising, writing from a progressive dispensational perspective (kingdom already, but not yet), argues the Old Testament reveals several passages of Scripture that are related to the kingdom. He states, "A key feature in Old Testament eschatology concerns a future kingdom that God will set up on this earth and which will be everlasting in duration."[40] He cites Daniel 2:34-35, 44; Isaiah 2:2-4; and Micah 4:1-8 as references. In addition, he mentions "Personal and national blessings are extended to Gentiles as well."[41]

Amillennialists interpret the "souls" that are beheaded (Rev. 20:4) as Christians who are in heaven reigning with Christ and waiting for His return. In regards to the first resurrection, this view teaches that believers will be resurrected twice. First, the believer will be resurrected at the moment of death into the presence of the Lord. Second, when Christ comes again (all the events happen at once–new heaven, new earth, resurrections); he will be bodily resurrected again. The second resurrection will be when the believer receives their eternal state. However, there are issues that need clarification with this method of interpretation. In comparing these passages with other Scriptures in the context of eschatological studies, there remains inconsistent information.

Exegetical Study of Revelation and Kingdom

There are four interpretational approaches to the book of Revela-

---

40   Gundry and Bock, 193.
41   Ibid.

tion. The historical, preterist, spiritual, and futuristic view. According to Feinberg, the historical "holds that the message gives the entire history of the church and pictures the antagonism of the forces of evil in the world against the church."[42] He writes, the preterist approach "interprets the greater prophecies as having been fulfilled in the struggles of the past, particularly in the conflict of the church with the Roman Empire."[43] The spiritual approach are those who "see in the book nothing more nor less than the final triumph of truth over error."[44] Feinberg identifies himself with the futuristic approach. He explains this view "maintains that all is future and prophetic from chapter four to the end."[45]

Revelation 20:1-10 can be summarized in the following way:

1. Satan will be literally bound for one thousand years and unable to be active on the earth. (1-3)
2. Positions of kingdom authority will be given to God's people. (4)
3. Martyred tribulation saints who have not received the mark of the beast or worshipped will be resurrected and reign with Christ for a thousand years. (4)
4. The "rest of the dead" shall come to life. (5)
5. Those who are a part of the first resurrection are priests of God and Christ and shall reign for a thousand years. (6)
6. At the end of the millennial (thousand years), Satan will be loosed and leads others astray only to be defeated by fire from heaven. (7-10)[46]

It has already been established that Christ's kingdom follows His return (Matt. 24:36-44; Zech. 14:4; Rev. 19:11-18). Those opponents of Jesus' literal reign on earth in the kingdom misinterpret Revelation 20:1-2. According to them, this passage is said to be obscure.

---

42 Feinberg, *Millennialism*, 181.
43 Ibid.
44 Ibid., 181-182.
45 Ibid., 182.
46 Vlach, 490.

Satan will be bound by an angel, but this is interpreted as having been fulfilled during the earthly ministry of Jesus. According to this view, there appears to be no purpose for the millennial. The question is proposed, if Jesus is going to be on earth, how can people sin? In response, while there will be a utopia on earth during the millennium with unparalleled conditions, yet man's sinful heart will lead him to follow Satan (Rev. 20:7-8). God's plan from the beginning was to reconcile sinful man by sending His Son who would die a substitutionary death on a cross, rise from the grave and provide justification (Rom. 4:25), ascend into heaven (Acts 1:11), and promise to come again (John 14:1-3). Ultimately, He gives eternal life to all who by faith believe on Him (Eph. 2:8-9; John 3:36; 5:24; Rom. 10:9-10).

Millennium (Kingdom) Conditions on Earth

What will the conditions be like on earth during the kingdom (millennial)? How different will it be when Jesus ushers in His anticipated kingdom? Will the church experience these changes? What are God's purposes for bringing His theocratic rule? Are there insights in both the Old and New Testaments concerning Christ's kingdom?

Pentecost has provided an excellent resource to the body of Christ that describes the conditions during the kingdom period. He has succeeded in deducing from the Scriptures "facts and features of this theocratic kingdom."[47] Commenting on Revelation 20:1-3, Pentecost describes the millennial age as being filled with divine righteousness. He declares, "It is evident that there can and will be no earthly theocratic kingdom apart from the personal manifested presence of the Lord Jesus Christ."[48] According to him, when the King comes, He establishes order and righteousness. This is a bold declaration refuting the kingdom now theology.

Christ will be called the "branch" (Isa. 4:2; 11:1; Jer. 23:5; 33:15; Zech. 3:8-9; 6:12-13), the Lord of Hosts (Isa. 24:23; 44:6), the Ancient of Days (Dan. 7:13), the Lord (Micah 4:7; Zech. 14:9), and Jehovah (Isa. 2:2-4; 7:14; 9:6; Jer. 3:17; 23:5-6; Ezek. 43:5-7; 44:1-2;

---

47 Pentecost, *Things to Come*, 476.
48 Ibid., 478.

Joel 3:21). During the kingdom, His rule and reign will be a theocracy. Other names Jesus will be called are the rod of Jesse (Isa. 11:1, 11), the Son of man (Dan. 7:13), and the King (Isa. 11:1-10; 33:17, 22; 44:6; Dan. 2:44; Obad. 17-21; Micah 4:1-8; Zech. 3:9-10; 14:16-17). As King, He will rule in authority and power.

Chester Woodring says, "The millennium will be the period of the full manifestation of the glory of the Lord Jesus Christ."[49] Both His humanity and deity will be manifested, according to Pentecost.[50] He shall sit on His throne.

His kingdom shall be characterized by a spiritual manifestation. Pentecost argues against the amillennial view. He says, "It is argued that the amillennialist envisions the kingdom as a "spiritual" kingdom and the premillennialist sees it as "carnal" or "material" only."[51] To clarify, he says, "Such presentation fails to distinguish between the spiritualized view of the millennium and the spiritual realities in the millennium, or between a spiritual kingdom and a spiritualized view of the kingdom."[52] His point being, premillennialists do not deny the spiritual presence and power of the King during the kingdom, but they do differentiate between a church age presently operating in the world with spiritual power from the Holy Spirit awaiting the physical presence and power of the King's return.

Oswald T. Allis writes, "The kingdom announced by John and Jesus was primarily and essentially a moral and spiritual kingdom.... He declared unto Pilate, 'My kingdom is not of this world' " (John xviii 36).[53] Righteousness and peace are descriptive of the kingdom period. Woodring writes, "only the 'righteous' are admitted to the kingdom; 'then shall the *righteous answer*' (Matt 25:37)."[54] Jesus, the King, will reign in righteousness. Those in the kingdom will experience His glory.

The kingdom will be characterized by truth (John 14:6) and ho-

---

49   Chester Woodring, "The Millennial Glory of Christ" (master's thesis, Dallas Theological Seminary, 1944), 67, quoted in Pentecost, *Things to Come*, 480.
50   Pentecost, *Things to Come*, 480-481.
51   Ibid., 482.
52   Ibid.
53   Oswald T. Allis, *Prophecy and the Church* (Philadelphia, PA: Presbyterian and Reformed Publishing Company, 1945, 69-71, quoted in Pentecost, *Things to Come*, 482.
54   Chester Woodring, "The Millennial Glory of Christ" (master's thesis, Dallas Theological Seminary, 1944), 113-116, quoted in Pentecost, *Things to Come*, 482.

liness (Isa. 35:8-10). Jesus will rule and reign over the nations in His holiness (Psa. 47:8-9). Believers will be filled with the Holy Spirit. Walvoord writes,

> It is evident from the Scriptures that all believers will be indwelt by the Holy Spirit in the millennium even as they are in the present age (Ezek. 36:27, 37:14; Jer. 31:33).... The filling of the Holy Spirit will be common in the millennium.... In contrast to present-day spiritual apathy, coldness, and worldliness, there will be spiritual fervor, love of God, holy joy, universal understanding of spiritual truth, and a wonderful fellowship of saints.... The emphasis will be on righteousness in life and on joy of spirit.[55]

This will be quite a contrast with today's condition. Anticipation of this kingdom should encourage believers to be faithful until the kingdom (millennium) comes.

Pentecost lists the conditions that describe the "greatness of the kingdom" (Dan. 7:27). It will be a time of peace (Isa. 2:4, 9:4-7), joy (Isa. 9:3-4; 65:25), comfort (Jer. 31:23-25), full knowledge (Isa. 11:1-2; Hab. 2:14), removal of curse (Gen. 3:17-19; Isa. 11:6-9; 65:25), sickness removed (Isa. 33:24; Jer. 30:17; Ezek. 34:16), protection (Isa. 41:8-14; Joel 3:16-17; Zech. 14:10-11), longevity (Isa. 65:20), reproduction (Jer. 30:20; 31:29; Ezek. 47:22), economic prosperity (Isa. 4:1; 65:21-23; Ezek. 34:26; Micah 4:1, 4; Zech. 8:11-12; 9:16-17; Amos 9:13-14), and unified worship (Isa. 45:23; 52:1; Zech. 13:2; 14:16).[56] God's majesty and authority will be established during the kingdom (millennial) reign. His government will be a theocracy. David will be co-regent in the kingdom (Ezek. 34:23-24). Pentecost explains, "There is no question but that the Lord Jesus Christ will reign in the theocratic kingdom on earth by virtue of the fact that He was born in David's line and possesses the royal and legal rights to the throne (Matt 1:1; Luke 1:32, 33)."[57] God's Word will be fulfilled.

What about the Old Testament saints? When will they be resur-

---

55   John Walvoord, *The Holy Spirit* (Grand Rapids, MI: Zondervan, 1958), 233-234.
56   Pentecost, *Things to Come*, 487-490.
57   Ibid., 498.

rected? How will all believers relate to each other in the kingdom? Is there a connection between Daniel 12:2 and Revelation 20:4?

Several precursors are seen from Daniel 12:1-3. This is before the kingdom begins. First, it will be a time of trouble, "And there shall be a time of trouble" (Dan. 11:36-45; 12:1). This is parallel of Revelation 12, which describes Satan's persecution on Israel (Rev. 12:13-17) and Michael's protection on God's people (Rev. 12:7).

The second precursor is found in Daniel 12:2. "And many of them that sleep in the dust of the earth shall awake, some to everlasting life, and some to shame and everlasting contempt." Feinberg writes, "All Old Testament saints are raised some time after the Tribulation, probably immediately after, according to Daniel 12:2, which follows the prophets word on the time of trouble."[58] He explains, "The resurrection of the Old Testament saints is cared for by Daniel 12:1-3 and is presupposed in Revelation 20:1-6."[59] Although he does not specifically identify this group as the Old Testament saints, Stephen Miller makes reference to this passage in Daniel 12:2. He concurs, "Believers will rise to enjoy 'everlasting life' in their new bodies and will reign with Christ (cf. Rev 20:4-6)."[60] However, John E. Goldingay avoids making the connection between Daniel 12:2 and Revelation 20:4 in his commentary.[61] Biblical evidence seems to affirm that the passage in Daniel and Revelation will be fulfilled at the beginning of the kingdom.

Pentecost clarifies any confusion. "This first resurrection in Revelation 20:6 cannot be made to apply to the church saints, for those here resurrected are those who have gone through the tribulation and thus would not be included in the body of Christ, since the resurrection of the church has preceded this."[62] Writing on Revelation 20:4, Walvoord identifies those with Christ. "One possibility is that the subject of the verb 'sat' includes Christ and all the saints related to Him including

---

58 Charles L. Feinberg, *Millennialism*, 184.
59 Ibid.
60 Stephen Miller, *The New American Commentary*, Vol. 18 (Nashville, TN: Broadman & Holman, 1994), 316-317.
61 John E. Goldingay, *Word Biblical Commentary*, Vol. 30 (Dallas, TX: Word Books Pub., 1989), 306-309.
62 Pentecost, *Things to Come*, 543.

both the church and Israel."⁶³ Explaining further he notes, "The most probable interpretation is that they are the twenty-four elders who are said to reign on the earth (5:10)."⁶⁴ He lists a parallel passage in Matthew 19:28, and concludes, "The privilege of reigning with Christ is not exclusively the reward of the church, but the righteous saints in general are given privileged places of service."⁶⁵

What changes will take place during the millennium kingdom? How different will the kingdom be than presently? The animal world will be restored. An investigation of the changes during the kingdom period shows that it is not spiritual but rather it will result in physical changes. McClain writes, "Both those who accept as inspired the Genesis account of man's original state in Eden (2:19) will have no difficulty in believing that God is able to restore these conditions in the coming Kingdom of His Son."⁶⁶ Speaking about the Old Testament prophets, McClain says, "They saw the future Kingdom penetrating and functioning in all the important realms of human life: spiritual, ethical, social, political, ecclesiastical, and physical."⁶⁷

According to Paul, the earth anticipates changes (Rom. 8:19-21). The timing on that event is debated. Some claim it will happen during the millennium, others place it after the kingdom period (Rev. 20-21). Grudem says, "In this renewed creation, there will be no more thorns or thistles, no more floods or droughts, no more deserts or uninhabitable jungles, no more earthquakes or tornadoes, no more poisonous snakes or bees that sting or mushrooms that kill."⁶⁸ A description of Isaiah 11:6-9 is as follows:

- "the wolf will dwell with the lamb" (v. 6)
- "the leopard will lie down with the kid" (young goat)(v. 6)
- "the calf and the young lion" will live together (v. 6)
- "the cow and the bear shall feed" (v. 7)

---

63   John Walvoord, *The Revelation of Jesus Christ* (Chicago, IL: Moody Press, 1966), 296.
64   Ibid., 296.
65   Walvoord, *The Revelation of Jesus Christ*, 299.
66   McClain, 239.
67   Ibid., 218.
68   Grudem, 836.

- "the lion shall eat straw like an ox" (v. 7)
- "the sucking child shall play on the hole of the asp"–play with poisonous snakes and not be harmed (v. 8)

Animals will be in perfect harmony. Isaiah 65:25 reads, "The wolf and the lamb shall feed together, and the lion shall eat straw like the bullock." Feinberg explains there are those who interpret Isaiah 9:6-9 from an amillennium perspective. According to him, Hoekema rejects this passage as the millennium kingdom; rather he suggests it takes place in the new earth.[69] Opposing Hoekema, McClain writes, "Those today who are belligerently opposed to the idea of a literal Kingdom of Christ on the earth are the scholars who either largely ignore the Old Testament or else dissolve in the acid of their 'spiritualization' those prophetic elements which are repugnant to them."[70]

The Church in the Kingdom

How will the church relate to the kingdom? What role will the church play? Are there any Scriptural references to the church and her function in the kingdom?

God has a purpose for His church in the kingdom. Vlach comments on the phrase the "thrones" found in Revelation 20:4. According to Vlach, "thrones" has the idea of the kingdom with positions of authority.[71] Since the term "thrones" is plural, he suggests the task may be carried out by more than one person. Rather than the interpretation that identifies it with the four and twenty elders, he believes it is more likely the armies that return with Christ at His second coming (Rev. 19:14, 19). The armies will be the church. He notes, "This group is the nearest antecedent of the 'they' in Revelation 20:4."[72] Vlach makes the connection between Revelation 2:26-27, Revelation 3:21, and Revelation 20:4 as the church. Jesus promises them positions of ruling over the nations with Him on His throne. Vlach explains, "National

---

69 Charles L. Feinberg, *Millennialism*, 339.
70 McClain, 496.
71 Vlach, 498.
72 Ibid.

entities will exist in the kingdom and they will be ruled over by the Messiah and His people. Isaiah 19:24-25 lists Egypt, Assyria, and Israel as nations in the kingdom."[73] Both Dillow and Vlach concur that Christ will delegate His reign to His followers over the nations because of their faithfulness in this present age.[74]

John Walvoord writes on the passage Revelation 2:26-29 in regards to being overcomers. "The word 'rule' (Greek-*poimanei*) means literally 'to shepherd.' Their rule will not be simply that of executing judgment, but also that of administering mercy and direction to those who are the sheep as contrasted to the goats (Matt. 25:31-46)."[75]

In His letter to the church of Thyatira, John inspired by the Holy Spirit writes,

> But that which ye have *already* hold fast till I come. And he that overcometh, and keepeth my works unto the end, to him will I give power over the nations: And he shall rule them with a rod of iron; as the vessels of a potter shall they be broken to shivers: even as I received of my Father (Rev. 2.25-27).

This was a promise Jesus gave to the church. This is an indicator that the church is not in the kingdom.

Another future promise that Jesus gave to the church is found in Revelation 3:21. "To him that overcometh will I grant to sit with me in my throne, even as I also overcame, and am set down with my Father in his throne." Vlach says, "The overcomer is one who 'will' (future tense) sit down with Jesus on His throne."[76] This promise will be fulfilled after Christ comes again and ushers in His kingdom. In the context of Revelation 3:21 and overcoming, Walvoord concurs as he writes, "In that future time when His sovereignty will be manifested to the entire world, those who put their trust in Him will reign with him as His bride and consort, as the ones who have identified themselves with Christ in this present age of grace."[77]

---

73   Vlach, 476.
74   Ibid., 130.
75   Walvoord, *The Revelation of Jesus Christ*, 77.
76   Vlach, 558.
77   Walvoord, *The Revelation of Jesus Christ*, 99.

These promises to the church should motivate every Christian to be faithful to the finish (2 Tim. 4:7-8). There are rewards to be given by the King. The King came the first time (Matt. 2:2). He fulfilled His purpose and promised to come again (John 14:1-3). Consequently, His kingdom has been temporarily postponed. However, presently, all the suffering, persecution, and afflictions will pale in comparison to reigning and serving with the King.

Kingdom of Satan

The devil has always desired to be worshipped (2 Thess. 2.4; Isa. 14; Ezek. 28). According to a lecture by DeYoung, that is the reason Satan was ejected from the third heaven to the second heaven (Eph. 2.2; Isa.14.12-15; Luke 10:18-19). He attempted to set up his eternal kingdom.

Because of pride in his heart, Lucifer fell from his exalted position in heaven. Apparently, at one time he was "perfect in beauty" (Ezek. 28:12). Chapter 28 of the book of Ezekiel begins with the judgment of the Prince of Tyrus or according to DeYoung, modern day Lebanon. However, a transition takes place beginning in verse twelve. It becomes very evident that the writer moves from the Prince of Tyrus to another one who is located in Eden (Ezek. 28:13), namely Lucifer. He was called the anointed cherub and set in the holy mountain of God–or the place of Eden, which is presently believed to be in the location of the temple mount. Furthermore, he was sinless at the time he had access to walk up and down in the "midst of the stone of fire" (Ezek. 28:14). According to Renald Showers, some Old Testament scholars believed that this phrase was a reference to the very presence of God.[78]

In addition, this can be supported because in the Old Testament, God's presence had been revealed through fire on occasion. This was clearly seen in Ezekiel Chapter One in the encounter Ezekiel had with the glory of God. Moses experienced God through the burning bush (Exod. 3:2).

Perfection was found in Lucifer from his creation until iniquity

---

78   Renald E. Showers, *Those Invisible Spirits Called Angels* (Friends of Israel Ministry, Inc., 1997), 78.

marred the angel (Ezek. 28:15). He sinned and consequently fell from his position (Ezek. 28:16). His sin resulted in his ejection from the third heaven (Ezek. 28:17; Eph. 2:2). This would lead him to implement a false kingdom. Ultimately, he will be cast out of the first heaven to the earth (Rev. 12:7-9). His final destination will be the lake of fire (Rev. 20:10). His kingdom will fall.

Isaiah Chapter 14 gives the reader some additional insight into what took place with Lucifer's fall. Isaiah speaks about Israel before the coming of the Messiah. However, the last chapters in Isaiah speak about the Messiah and His messianic kingdom.

At the beginning of Chapter 14 and throughout the first eleven verses, Isaiah seemed to be referencing a proud ruler in Babylon. Yet, the Holy Spirit inspired Isaiah from verse fourteen to speak about another one, namely an angel. "How art thou fallen from heaven, O Lucifer, son of the morning" (Isa. 14:12). The root of Lucifer's problem was arrogant pride. If one could trace the downward fall of Lucifer, perhaps it would lead to his desire to have dominion over the earth including man. Because of Lucifer's high rank and perfection, he desired to be like God and take control. But God gave that authority to His creation made in His image (Gen. 1:26-28).

DeYoung describes Lucifer as being furious. Thus, he plotted and planned a way to get authority and dominion over the delegated authority given to man. Therefore, he used deception through schemes and lies about God and His Word (Gen 3.1-15). In just a short while, Satan had instigated the overthrow of a theocracy into a Satanocracy.[79] According to Showers, "the term theocracy literally means rule of God and refers to the form of government in which the rule of God is administered by a representative."[80] God's plan allowed it to take place. This will remain until Jesus comes again and establishes His kingdom upon the earth (Rev. 20:1-10). Then, once again, there will be a theocracy.

Satan created more damage when he fell. Other angels rebelled against God and followed him. Some of the angels were confined to "hell." According to Showers, the ancient world differentiated

---

79   Showers, *Those Invisible Spirits Called Angels*, 84.
80   Ibid.

between the place hades and tartarus.[81] Evidentially, it was a place of torment. Another conclusion is their "sin" must have been different than Lucifer's seeing the fact that he was not confined to that place. Finally, tartarus was "reserved unto judgment" (2 Pet. 2:4). Satan's kingdom includes these fallen angels.

Other Scriptures indicate Satan "and the evil angel's destination" are judgment (Matt. 25:41; Rev. 12:7-9); furthermore, Satan was said to be ruler over the evil angels (Mark 12:24-26). After Jesus was led into the wilderness during His temptation by Satan, he went to the top of a mountain. The devil showed Him all the "kingdoms of the world" and attempted to give them to Jesus if He would worship him. How could he do that? God's sovereignty allowed Satan the kingdoms of the world at the fall of man in the garden (Luke 4:5-6).

Satan and his demonic hordes of hell will be overthrown. However, first, he will empower the person of the Antichrist (2 Thess. 2:1-4; Matt. 24:15; Dan. 9:27). He and his false prophet will mislead and make war with the tribulation saints (Rev. 13:1-18). A false apostate church and a united world government, and their last attempt for control will come to an end (Rev. 17:20). "The KING of KINGS and LORD of LORDS" will come again in glory and power and throw the Antichrist and the false prophet into the lake of fire to be tormented forever (Rev. 19:11-20).

Satan knows his time is short (Rev. 12:12). But first, Jesus will come again in the event called the rapture of the church (1 Thess. 4:16-17). Then, after seven years of tribulation, He will return in glory and power, and fight the final war of Armageddon (Rev. 19:11-16; Matt. 24:36-44; Luke 21:24-28; Zech. 14:1-4). His eternal kingdom will be established on earth (Rev. 20:1-9) and throughout eternity (Rev. 21-22). God will rule and reign on the earth in a theocracy. Satan will be thrown into the lake of fire with the false prophet and the beast to be tormented forever (Rev. 20:10). This fits into God's plan from eternity past to eternity future.

---

81   Showers, 89.

Kingdom of Nimrod

The origin of false religion can be traced back to the book of Genesis with Nimrod who was the grandson of Noah. He led a revolt against God and built his "kingdom" on the plains of Shinar (Gen. 10:10). According to DeYoung's lecture, the Scripture reveals his hideous plan of false worship. From the Tower of Babel to Pergamos and finally to Rome, and then back to Babylon, the false church has been established. "Babylon the great, the mother of harlots and of the abominations of the earth" (Rev. 17:5). John wrote describing the false church and its judgment.

In the letter to the church of Pergamos, the Lord Jesus spoke of "Satan's seat" (Rev 2.13), the doctrine of Balaam, and the Nicolaitanes. While on a Bible prophecy trip in Rome, DeYoung spoke about the progression of the Babylonian cult "Satan's seat" that started in Genesis and ends in Revelation. He explained the following: Nimrod led a revolt against the Lord by building a tower called the "tower of Babel" (Gen. 11). It was a pagan temple built in direct rebellion toward the command of God to be fruitful and multiply. Instead of obeying, Nimrod started the false religion. Consequently, God confused the people's language and scattered them on the face of the earth. According to DeYoung, Nimrod married Semiramis who was called the "queen of heaven" in Jeremiah 44:17. They had a son named Tammuz. Ezekiel mentions him in Ezekiel 8:14. This was a mother-son cult. Tradition claims that he died from a wild boar attack and then came back to life again. DeYoung said this false religion of worship started in Babylon and crossed into Turkey into the church of Pergamos and will travel to Rome where the Antichrist will set up his headquarters. Later, he will move to the temple and set up his image (Rev. 13:15-18), and then to Babylon (2 Thess. 2:4-5; Rev. 17-18). Religious Babylon will come to its end when the beast turns on it. Satan's kingdom will be overthrown when he is cast into the lake of fire with the beast and the false prophet to be tormented forever (Rev. 20:10).

Jesus' kingdom will stand forever. God's Word declares it (Luke 1:32-33; Dan. 7:13-14). He will sit on the throne. All will worship Him. Paul writes, "That at the name of Jesus every knee should bow, of things in heaven, and things in earth, and things under the earth;

and that every tongue should confess that Jesus Christ is Lord, to the glory of God the Father." (Phil. 2:10-11).

Worship in the Kingdom (Ezekiel's – Messiah's Temple)

How will the church participate in the kingdom? Will the believing Jews worship their Messiah? What differences will there be between the millennial temple and the previous ones? Why will there be sacrifices during the millennium? Will Messiah's temple remain on earth forever? Will many of the prophecies concerning Jesus be fulfilled during this time?

There will be worship in the kingdom. Messiah's temple will be built. It is referred to as Ezekiel's temple or the Messiah's temple. The glory of the Lord will return to the temple since its departure (Ezek. 8-11; 43:2). "The eastern gate that overlooks the Kidron Valley today is closed as it has been since the Crusades, nearly a thousand years ago."[82] Cooper notes that Muslims believe that this gate (today it's called the Golden Gate–Eastern gate) will be the place of final judgment, and call it the gate of heaven and hell.[83]

According to DeYoung, from Chapters 40 to 46 in Ezekiel, there are at least 202 verses that deal with this futuristic temple. Jesus will build this temple. The book of Zechariah sheds some light in regards to this temple. "Behold the man whose name is The BRANCH; and he shall grow up out of his place, and he shall build the temple of the Lord" (Zech. 6.12).

There are three major interpretations of Ezekiel 40-48, according to Vlach.[84] The first view is historical which interprets this as being fulfilled with the return of the remnant from exile and the rebuilding of the temple before Christ. The second view interprets this as being spiritually fulfilled in Jesus and the church. The third view interprets this as a coming literal temple.[85] Leslie C. Allen does not write from the literal view of the coming of the temple in the millennium

---

82   Lamar Cooper, Sr., *The New American Commentary*, Vol. 17 (Broadman and Holman, 1994), 388.
83   Ibid.
84   Vlach, 203.
85   Ibid.

kingdom.[86] This writer concurs with the literal view, which predicts a future temple where Jesus rules and reigns as described in Ezekiel.

The answer to the topography changes in Jerusalem, when Jesus comes again, can be found by searching the passage of Zechariah 14. On that day (the day of the Lord), when all the armies of the world shall come against Jerusalem (Zech. 14:2), Jesus will return and His feet will land on the Mt. of Olives. The mountain will cleave or split into, thus changing the geographic structure of the area (Ezek. 14:4).

The sacrificial system will be reinstituted (Ezek. 45). The sacrifices will be only in remembrance of Jesus since He has satisfied the holy demands of a holy God (1 John 2:2; Heb. 9:28). The purpose will be to restore fellowship for the Jews living in the millennial period with earthly bodies. Salvation for all humanity is accomplished by "grace alone" through "faith alone" in "Christ alone" (Eph. 2:8-9). However, after conversion, fellowship with God becomes the great need for the believer. John wrote to believers describing how Christians can walk with the Lord on a daily basis.

Cooper writes, "Since the church will be taken out of the world, or raptured, prior to the tribulation (Rev 4:1), the tribulation will be the era of conversion for Israel (Rev. 7:1ff.), and the millennium will afford them the opportunity to reinstate their covenant to celebrate and commemorate the redemptive work of Jesus the Messiah."[87] Both Jews and the church will be present during the kingdom period. John Schmitt explains, "Since Jerusalem will be the center of world government in the kingdom and the Temple will be the place of Messiah's throne, we may be looking at a building complex that will be our future ministry site."[88] He clarifies, "The temple is important because Christians will worship there during Christ's reign on earth."[89] The church is presently preparing for the kingdom to come and for worship to be moved from the church building to the temple building. Even though, it is understood that true worship is done in the heart not necessarily confined to a building.

---

86 Leslie C. Allen, *Word Biblical Commentary*. Vol. 29 (Dallas, TX: Word Books Pub., 1990), 212-270.
87 Cooper, 381.
88 John Schmitt and Carl Laney, *Messiah's Coming Temple* (Grand Rapids, MI: Kregal Publishing, 2004), 17.
89 Ibid., 20.

In Messiah's temple, King David will be co-regent as prince (Ezek. 45:22; 34:23-24). DeYoung said in a lecture that in Messiah's temple on the Jewish feast of Yom Kippur, or the day of atonement, Jesus will take those Jews that have been preserved in Petra into the temple and they will see Him and be saved (Isa. 63:1-4; Rev. 12:6, 14; Matt 24:16; Rom. 11:25-26; Zech. 13:8-9). Zechariah wrote that the Jews will be saved in a day (Zech. 3:9).

Ezekiel's prophecy was given while he was exiled in Babylon. He was taken in 597 BC by Nebuchadnezzar. While training for the priesthood, Ezekiel was taught the role of the priest in the temple. This included detailed instructions for sacrifices in the temple, health issues, law and justice, financial administration, construction and maintenance, and worship. Before his ministry officially began, he saw the glory of God. This is recorded in Chapter One. Consequently, he became a watchman upon the wall. DeYoung breaks the book into two sections. The first 32 chapters can be described as "God's Retribution," and Chapters 33-48, as "God's Restoration."

God's plan is to bring Israel back to their homeland (Ezek. 33-37), which has been partially fulfilled. It is continuing today. God's plan for Israel in the future is described in Scripture. Jesus will return for His church (1 Cor. 15:51-54). A covenant will be confirmed by the Antichrist (Dan. 9:27). This will take place at the beginning of tribulation during a time of peace for Israel (1 Thess. 5:2-3). Israel will be attacked by an alignment of nations (Ezek. 38-39), who will be destroyed by God. Then, God gave Ezekiel a detailed description of the Messiah's temple (Ezek. 40-48).

In studying Ezekiel's temple, there are significant differences. The Outer Court structure of Ezekiel's temple consists of the outer wall (Ezek. 40:5), the eastern gate (40:6-14, 16), northern gate (40:20-22), southern gate (40:24-26), lower pavement (40:18), chambers of the lower pavement (40:17), corner kitchens (46:21-24), and outer court (40:15, 19, 23, 27). Conversely, the inner court's detail includes the northern gate (40:35-43), eastern gate (40:32-34), southern gate (40:28-31), inner court dimensions (40:47), chambers of inner court (40:44-46), chambers for the temple (40:45), chamber for the altar (40:46), temple building (40:48-41:11, 13-26), separate place (41:21), priest's chamber (42:1-14), kitchens for the priest's chambers (46:19-

20), and altar (43:13-17).

God gave Ezekiel a vision as He carried him to the land of Israel (40:2-3). Then, an angel appeared; DeYoung said in a lecture, it could be the angel of the Lord or a pre-incarnate Christ (40:3). He informed Ezekiel to be ready to look and then tell what he saw about Israel. What did he see? There was a wall that surrounded the entire temple (40:5). Also, there appeared the outer court and three gates, along with the inner court and three gates. The inner court was on a higher level and included a place for the burnt offering, sin offering, and guilt offering (40:27-47). Then Ezekiel saw the most holy place in the temple (40:48-41:26). With detail, he noted the side chambers (three floors of rooms) and a large building behind the temple. The interior of the temple was revealed. Designated places for the priest to eat the sacrifices and for storing their clothing were seen (42:1-13). Overall, one side of the temple measured about one mile, giving the estimated size of the temple approximately one square mile (42:15-20; 45:1-2).

The announcement was made that the temple was to be holy (43:6-12). Burnt offerings along with peace offerings were to be demonstrated on the altar (43:13-27). Specific instructions were given to shut the eastern gate (44:1-3). A prince was introduced to Ezekiel (44:3). While some claim this to be the Messiah, it becomes obvious that this is unlikely because whoever it is needs to offer a sin offering (45:22). Jesus does not need a sin offering. Levites were given the responsibility of overseeing the duties of the temple with one of their primary tasks being teaching the people (44:23). Ezekiel was told the priest shall be supported by being allotted a sacred area of land within the eight square miles (45:1-8). Furthermore, the prince David's portion (34:24) of land stretched out about eight miles beyond the priest's portion (43:7). Since the people shall give to him, the prince shall be responsible for providing the sacrifice (45:13-17). The feast of tabernacles and the feast of Passover will be celebrated in the Messiah's temple (46:1-16), along with the year of jubilee (46:17). All of this is in remembrance of the sacrifice of Jesus.

Then Ezekiel saw a river flowing from the temple traveling eastward (47:1-12). At first, it is only a trickle and then it becomes a deep river. Trees can be seen growing on the banks of this river. The sweetened water will turn the Dead Sea into a sea full of fish that are living (47:8-10). However, some of the swampy marshes will remain salty (47:11). According to J. Vernon McGee's commentary on Ezekiel, the water described in Ezekiel 47 is a type of the Holy Spirit.[90] He makes mention of the "waters to swim in" indicate the fullness of the Spirit; furthermore, he suggested this text looks ahead to the day when God pours out His Spirit upon the Jews.

Toward the end of Ezekiel's vision, the Lord gave directions as to how the land will be distributed among the twelve tribes of Israel (Ezek. 47:13-48:35). Israel will possess all the land that God had promised Abraham (Deut. 30). Joseph will be given two portions (Ezek. 47:13). Seven tribes will be given land north of the temple. These include: Dan (see Rev. 7:4), Asher, Naphtali, Manasseh, Ephraim, Reuben, and Judah (Ezek. 48:1-7). Conversely, five tribes will be given land south of the temple (Ezek. 48:23-29). These include Benjamin, Simeon, Issachar, Zebulun, and Gad. And finally, Ezekiel was told there were three gates to each side of the city which would be named after each of the tribes including Levi and Joseph who represented Ephraim and Manasseh (Ezek. 48:31-34).

What is going to be missing in this futuristic temple that was evident in the other temples? John Schmitt and Carl Laney mentioned eight different articles that will be missing in Ezekiel's temple, or Messiah's Temple.[91]

The first item listed was the wall of partition. In the other temples, a wall about 4½ feet high, according to Josephus, separated the inner court and the outer court of the temple.[92] However, through the sacrificial death of Jesus, the wall has been broken down, thus allowing both the Jews and the Gentiles to become one body in Christ (Eph. 2:14). Secondly, there will not be the court of women, which permitted women from entering the inner court. Through the finished works of Calvary, both men and women become one in Christ (Gal. 3:27-28).

Third, the bronze laver, used by the priests for personal cleansing, will be absent. Perhaps the reason is because of the cleansing power of

---

[90] Vernon J. McGee, *Thru the Bible*, Vol. 3 (Nashville, TN: Thomas Nelson, 1982), 522.
[91] Schmitt and Laney, *Messiah's Coming Temple*, 181-191.
[92] Ibid, 183.

the blood of Jesus (1 John 1:7, 9; Titus 3:5-6). Fourth, the lampstand (menorah), or candlestick, is missing in the new temple for the millennium. Why? Jesus said He was the light of the world (John 8:12; John 1:4). Fifth, there is no mention of the table of showbread. The reason the bread will not be needed is because Jesus is "the bread of life" (John 6:35). Sixth, during the millennial kingdom, when Jesus is ruling and reigning, the altar of incense will be missing. The altar of incense demonstrated symbolically the prayers of God's people and pointed to Jesus because He is the great high priest who ever lives to make intercession for the saints (Heb. 7:25). Seventh, because the veil was torn from top to bottom when Jesus died on the cross, it will not be needed in the Messiah's temple. Eighth, and the last of the missing elements in this futuristic temple, will be the Ark of the Covenant. Who needs the replica of the real thing? Jesus is the real thing and He will fill the temple with His presence (Ezek. 43:5-7).

The glory of the Lord will return again as previously mentioned (Ezek. 43:4). Ezekiel describes what will take place next. "And he said unto me, Son of man, the place of my throne, and the place of the soles of my feet, where I will dwell in the midst of the children of Israel forever" (43:7). According to DeYoung, this indicates Messiah's temple will stand in Jerusalem forever (37:26, 28).

He explains, this passage by Ezekiel is the foretelling of the day that Jesus will return from Petra to Jerusalem after rescuing the Jewish people who have been preserved in a "place prepared of God" (Isa. 63:1-3; Rev. 12:6; Matt. 24:16). This event will follow the battle of Armageddon, which will be fought in the valley of Jezreel. The temple will be rebuilt (Zech. 6:12-13), and Jesus will take His place on His throne (Ezek. 43:7). "It is at this time that the Lord Jesus Christ fulfills the Jewish Feast Day of Yom Kippur."[93] He concludes the devotion by saying believers need to know this information since the church will be ruling and reigning with the Lord Jesus during the kingdom.

Another significant difference in the Messiah's Temple will be the change in the altar. Those offering a sacrifice on the altar will be

---

93   Jimmy DeYoung, "Prophetic Prospective Daily Devotional: Ezekiel 48:1," Prophecy Today, http://devotional.prophecytoday.com/search/label/Ezekiel (accessed January 14, 2018).

walking toward the east not toward the south as they did in the previous temples.[94] Rather, they will be approaching the altar from the east side moving in the direction where Jesus will be seated upon His throne. In the other temples, the ramp would have been going from the south up to the north; however, in the new temple, the stairs are going to be looking to the east, thus the stairs will be coming from the west up to the altar. God had them build the steps leading from the south to the north instead of the east to the west in the temples built previously so that they would not worship the sun as it was going down in the west or coming up in the morning in the east.

Normally, the word used to describe the altar in the Bible was *mizbach,* but in Ezekiel 43:15-16, the Hebrew word is *ariel.*[95] Interesting to note, the root meaning of this word *ariel* means "lion of God."[96] Jesus will be called the "lion from the tribe of Judah" (Rev. 5:5). In Ezekiel's temple, the altar will be named in Messiah's honor. The priest will walk up the stairs to the top of the altar, *ariel* (lion of God), and look into the Holy of Holies at Jesus who will be on His throne as the KING of KINGS and LORD of LORDS, and the lion from the tribe of Judah.

While there will be a temple upon the earth during the kingdom period (millennium) and throughout eternity future (Ezek. 37:26, 28), there will not be any need for a temple in the New Jerusalem (Rev. 21:22). The earthly temple and the heavenly New Jerusalem appear to be two different places for worship in eternity future. In the book of Daniel, in Chapter Seven, Daniel described a kingdom that will not be destroyed but is everlasting and will be given to Jesus (Dan. 7:13-14). This apparently will include the earthly Messiah's temple or the one that Ezekiel described. Moreover, John wrote that in the New Jerusalem there will be no need for a temple—for Jesus will be the temple (Rev. 21:22). It seems like the New Jerusalem will be suspended above the new earth where Messiah's temple will be located. So one would conclude that there will be a temple on earth because the Word of God indicates it will be forever, whereas, there will not be a temple in the New Jerusalem. There is no contradiction here at all.

---

94 Schmitt and Laney, *Messiah's Coming Temple*, 190-191.
95 Ibid.
96 Ibid., 191.

Life in the Kingdom (Millennium)

How long will people live in the kingdom? Will death take place? Who will go into the kingdom? Can there be a contrast and comparison with life today?

Isaiah writes, "For, behold, I create new heavens and a new earth: and the former shall not be remembered, nor come into mind" (Isa. 65:17). What will be the conditions of this kingdom to come?

1. there will be Joy in Jerusalem (Isa. 65:19)
2. there will be no weeping or crying (Isa. 65:19)
3. no babies or infants will die (Isa. 65:20)
4. elderly people will not die young but will live out their lives (Isa. 65:20)
5. a person that dies at 100 will be considered cursed (Isa. 65:20)
6. people will build and live in their houses (Isa. 65:21)
7. those who plant vineyards will eat out of them (Isa. 65:21)
8. people will work and enjoy the fruit of their labor (Isa. 65:22)
9. animals will live together in harmony (Isa. 65:25)[97]

Compared to this fallen world, conditions will be more favorable. Grudem explains, "There will be no more infants who die in infancy, and no more old men die prematurely, something far different from this present age. However, death and sin will still be present, for the child who is one hundred years old shall die, and the sinner who is one hundred years old 'shall be accursed.'"[98] He is correct in analyzing Isaiah's prophetic insights.

Opponents of the futuristic "millennial kingdom" interpretation include John Watts. He summarizes this passage in Isaiah. "In 65:1-16, Yahweh addresses his court and those in Jerusalem who have opposed his vision. In 65:17-66:5, he speaks impersonally about his goals for Jerusalem without reference to either his opponents or his

---

97 Vlach, 173-174.
98 Grudem, 1128.

servants."⁹⁹ There is no mention of future eschatological fulfillments in the millennial kingdom. Others who oppose his view connect Isaiah 65:17-25 with Revelation 20.

Comparing Isaiah's passage (Isa. 65:17-25) with the "new heaven and the new earth" found in Revelation 21:1, it seems that the former is not described as being free of the presence of sin and yet the latter indicates sin will be eradicated. McClain says,

> It is apparent, therefore, that Isaiah saw together on the screen of prophecy both the Millennial Kingdom and the Eternal Kingdom; but he expands in detail the former because it is the 'nearest–coming' event and leaves the latter for fuller description in a later New Testament revelation.[100]

During the millennial kingdom, longevity of life will be prevalent. The lifespan today is seventy to eighty years (Psa. 90:10). However, in the millennial kingdom, one hundred years will be normal (Isa. 65:20). But in the new heaven and earth John describes, there will be no more death (Rev. 21:4). So what is the difference in Isaiah's prophecy and John's prophecy in Revelation? Vlach explains, "The best view is the conditions of Isaiah 65:20 occur in an *intermediate kingdom* that comes between our present era and the eternal state."[101] John sees the chronological events unfolding from Revelation Chapter 20 to Revelation Chapter 21. There is a progression of details as the future is being explained.

So, does Isaiah 65:17-25 describe the millennial kingdom or the eternal kingdom found in Revelation 21 and 22? Russell Moore argues, "Isaiah 65:17-21 seems to 'conflate the new heavens and the new earth' with an intermediate stage of the Kingdom in which death and rebellion are still present."[102] According to him, it is an initial phase of the kingdom. Vlach concurs, but clarifies. Although there

---

99   John D. Watts, *Word Biblical Commentary*, Vol. 25 (Waco, TX: Word Books, 1987), 338.
100   McClain, 138.
101   Vlach, 175.
102   Russell D. Moore, *The Kingdom of Christ: The New Evangelical Perspective* (Wheaton, IL: Crossway, 2004), 64, quoted in Vlach, 523.

are similarities, there are distinctive differences. He notes, in the millennium, Jesus rules and reigns, but in the eternal kingdom both the Father and the Son rule (1 Cor. 15:24-28). In the millennium, the nations are subject to Christ but still have death and sin to combat (Zech. 14:16-19; Isa. 65:20). In the eternal kingdom, sin and death will be abolished (Rev. 21:4, 8, 27). The curse will be lifted in its final state in the eternal kingdom (Isa. 30:23; 35:1-2; 35:7; Rev. 22:2). Jerusalem will be enlarged in the eternal kingdom (Rev. 21:10-21). An investigation of the two passages reveals some similarities but also some distinct differences.

Will there be a temple in the eternal kingdom? Vlach explains there will be a temple in the millennial kingdom (Ezek. 40-48). According to him, there will not be a temple in the eternal kingdom.[103] As noted earlier, DeYoung teaches the temple on earth will remain forever based on Ezekiel 37:26 and 28. Yet, he recognizes there will not be any need for a temple in the New Jerusalem because Jesus is the temple (Rev. 21:22). He interprets Isaiah 65:17-19 as eternity future and Isaiah 65:20-25 as the kingdom period in eternity future. His devotion shares "The birth of children in the Kingdom who will be 'children' until one hundred years of age. By the way, these children will be born to those, in physical bodies, who trust in Jesus Christ during the Tribulation Period and enter the Kingdom."[104] He continues, "At one hundred these 'children' must receive Jesus as their Saviour or they will be 'accursed' and sent to 'hades' to await their sentencing into the eternal 'Lake of Fire' at the Great White Throne (Rev. 20:11-15)."[105] God's plan is that all be forgiven through the blood of Jesus, His Son (Eph. 1:7; 1 Pet. 1:18-19; Heb. 9:22; Rev. 1:5).

What will happen to this earth during the millennial kingdom? How will it change? Has this already taken place? When is it projected? What goals are in the mind of God?

God made the heavens and the earth in the beginning and it was "very good" (Gen. 1:1-31). Due to the fall of man's sin, creation became cursed by death and decay (Gen. 3). Even creation longs

---

103   Vlach, 526-527.
104   Jimmy DeYoung, "Prophetic Prospective Daily Devotional: Isaiah 65:17," Prophecy Today, http://devotional.prophecytoday.com/search/label/Isaiah (accessed December 7, 2018).
105   Ibid.

for restoration. Paul wrote, "For we know that the whole creation groaneth and travaileth in pain together until now" (Rom. 8:22). Both the believer's body and the earth waits for that transformation and redemption (Rom. 8:23). In connection with the new heaven and the new earth, there are differences of opinion on the specific process God will use. Further discussion of this subject will be addressed in more detail in the following chapter.

Who will enter the millennial kingdom? Will it be for the unbeliever or just believers? Will these be Jews or Gentiles? Is the church included? What will be God's purpose?

The context of Matthew 24 and 25 has already been established as the tribulation period. The seal, trumpet, and vial judgments lead up to the second coming of Christ (Matt. 24:29-30). Consequently, the final battle of Armageddon takes place and prepares the earth for the millennial kingdom. Toussaint writes, "The closing words of the Olivet Discourse concern the judgment of the nations, the last event before the kingdom on earth is established."[106] He expounds his thoughts, "Since all of the ungodly Jews will be removed from the earth at the end of the tribulation (Zechariah 13:8-9), the sheep and goats must include 'all the nations' ... living on the earth at this time."[107] Discussing the meaning of the text concerning entrance into the kingdom, Toussaint says, "The criterion is the treatment of the Jewish evangelists in the tribulation (Matt. 25:40, 45)."[108] The unbelieving Gentiles will go into eternal punishment.

Jesus is not teaching that good works gets a person into heaven. Rather, He is reminding those that faith in Him is the only way, which results in good works (John 3:17-19; 5:24; 14:6). Paul taught the same doctrine (Eph. 2:8-10; Phil. 2:13; Titus 3:5-6).

Pentecost says, "The Gentile nations must be judged to determine who from among the living Gentiles will be accepted into His kingdom and who will be rejected."[109] Jesus describes this in the judgment of the sheep and goats (Matt. 25:31-46).

Who will go into the kingdom? Pentecost explains that no un-

---

106   Toussaint, 288.
107   Ibid., 291.
108   Ibid.
109   Dwight J. Pentecost, *Words and Works of Jesus Christ* (Grand Rapids, MI: Zondervan, 1981), 409.

saved person can enter His millennial kingdom.[110] According to him, that is why it will be necessary to separate the saved from the unsaved. Israel will be judged and then the nation will stand before Jesus (Matt. 25:32). He adds that this will be a "judgment of individuals and not of nations."[111] The phrase "the least of these my brethren" may refer to Israel, the 144,000 of Revelation 7.[112] Vlach concurs, and explains, "When Jesus comes with His kingdom, His initial action is to remove 'all stumbling blocks,' i.e. all non-believers from His newly established kingdom. This is consistent with Matthew 25:31-46."[113]

Blomberg interprets this passage from a different perspective. He agrees with Calvin that this is a picture of all humanity standing before Jesus at judgment day.[114] He writes, "No mention is made of those who died before Christ's return, but it would be natural to view this judgment as the same event as depicted in 1 Corinthians 15:51-57 and Revelation 20:4, in which all God's people of every era, including those already dead, are resurrected and/or given their new bodies."[115] Blomberg's remarks are both scripturally and theologically problematic. First, he confuses the rapture with the second coming of Christ, which is discussed in "The King's Evacuation of the Church Before the Kingdom." Second, he is mistaken with his eschatological assessment of the Great White Throne Judgment, which is for unbelievers (Rev. 20:11-15). The general resurrection view has been debated and concluded to be wrong in this chapter.

McClain argues Blomberg's doctrine. Discussing the passage in Matthew 25:31-46, McClain writes in opposition to it. He refutes it by saying,

> For those who hold to both the inspiration and intelligibility of Scripture, it should be clear that here we have no final judgment of the wicked dead, but a judgment of living nations; a judgment on earth, not in the heaven; an assize convened at the beginning of

---

110 Pentecost, *Words and Works of Jesus Christ*, 409.
111 Ibid.
112 Ibid., 410.
113 Vlach, 329.
114 Blomberg, 376.
115 Ibid.

the Millennial Kingdom of God, not as its close (cf. Rev. 20:1-15 and numerous texts already cited from Old Testament prophecy).[116]

McClain has revealed the flaws in Blomberg's conclusions. Staying consistent with the proper interpretation establishes unification from Genesis to Revelation.

Who will enter the kingdom? Toussaint clarifies, "The kingdom will include the resurrected saints of the Old Testament, the church (Colossians 1:13, 3:4; 2 Pet. 1:10-11), and the righteous people living at the time of the judgment of the nations."[117] Pentecost concurs as he discusses God's purpose. "God's purpose, then, is to populate the millennial kingdom by bringing a host from among Israel and the Gentile nations to Himself."[118] The church disappears during the tribulation in heaven, but reappears during the kingdom.

Both Jews and Gentiles will enter the kingdom from the tribulation in mortal bodies with the capability to reproduce. However, the church saints will have already received their glorified bodies (1 Cor. 15), and will be unable to reproduce. This explains the passages in Isaiah 65 and Revelation 20, and confirms what the post-tribulation view finds difficult to explain. This is another reliable reason for the body of Christ to teach "Church Now, Kingdom Later."

These terrestrial phenomena that are predicted in the millennial kingdom have not occurred in the present. Therefore, it must be understood that the kingdom foretold by the prophets will be in the future. The observational conclusion is the church is not in the kingdom now, but rather it will be later. This can be derived by two main evidences. First, if one interprets the Bible literally then it becomes obvious these supernatural transformations are missing. Second, there is both clarity and continuity between the Old and New Testaments in these prophetic passages in Isaiah and Revelation, along with other revealed truth.

---

116 McClain, 355.
117 Toussaint, 289.
118 Pentecost, *Things to Come*, 238.

Questions for Review and Discusssion

1. What does millennium mean?
2. Who will enter the millennial kingdom (see Matt. 25; Rev. 19; Zech. 13-14, etc.)?
3. Read and write a brief outline of Revelation 20, listing the different events that occur during the 1000-year period.
4. What are the three main views of the millennium?
5. Describe each view briefly.
6. What are the four different approaches to understanding and interpreting the book of Revelation?
7. What will the conditions on earth be like during the millennial kingdom? Will people die?
8. Write a brief outline of Isaiah 11:6-9, including Isaiah 65:17-25.
9. What role will the church have in the kingdom?
10. Discuss the kingdom of Satan.
11. Discuss the kingdom of Nimrod.
12. How will Messiah's temple be different than all other temples?
13. List the chapters and verses that relate to the millennial temple that Messiah will build.

Chapter Six

The King's Destination of the Earthly and Eternal Kingdom (Rev. 21-22)

What difference will there be in the eternal kingdom as opposed to the intermediate kingdom? How will the church participate in the New Jerusalem? Is God going to totally destroy the earth with fire or just renovate it? When will this take place?

In a description of the Great White Judgment, John writes, "I saw a great white throne and him that sat on it, from whose face the earth and the heaven fled away; and there was no place for them" (Rev. 20:11). This will be a time for unbelievers to be sentenced to the lake of fire (Rev. 20:15). Walvoord says, "The time is clearly at the end of the millennium in contrast to the other judgments which precede the millennium."[1]

In concurring with Walvoord, Fienberg explains the correct interpretation. Fienberg writing in opposition to the amillennialist view on this passage in Revelation 20:11 makes a valid point. He says, "It is impossible, so goes the objection, for all that to happen before the alleged Millennium. Premillennialists do not place this before the Millennium, but after it."[2] Fienberg refutes the opposing views by connecting the chronological events.

---

1   Walvoord, *Revelation of Jesus Christ*, 305.
2   Charles L. Feinberg, *Millennialism*, 317.

Walvoord explains the timing of the events that take place. "The most natural interpretation of the fact that the earth and the heaven flee away is that the present earth and heaven are destroyed and will be replaced by the new heaven and new earth."[3] According to him, the new heavens and earth will not be renovated but rather re-made.

Connecting the two passages together (Rev. 20:14; 21:1); John saw the new heaven and earth. "And I saw a new heaven and a new earth: for the first heaven and the first earth were passed away; and there was no more sea" (Rev. 21:1). Commenting on these verses, Walvoord concludes, "The new heaven and new earth presented here are evidently not simply the old heaven and the earth renovated, but an act of new creation."[4] Scholars like Walvoord use 2 Peter 3:10 to interpret the event. He explains, "The fact that millennial truths are mentioned in the same context in all three of these major references has often confused expositors. However, it is a common principle in prophecy to bring together events that are distantly related chronologically, such as frequent reference to the first and second comings of Christ."[5] Peter describes this prophetic scene.

> But the day of the Lord will come as a thief in the night; in which the heavens will pass away with a great noise, and the elements shall melt with fervent heat, the earth also and the works that are therein shall be burned up (2 Pet 3:10).

Richard Bauckham suggests there are three different interpretations of the word "the heavenly bodies be dissolved in the heat"– στοιχεια (2 Pet. 3:10).[6] The first view includes all the physical things burned: water, air, fire, and earth. The second view includes the heavenly bodies: sun, moon, stars. The third view is the angelic powers. He suggests the more important matter. "The apocalyptic imagery which follows depicts not simply the dissolution of the cosmos, but more

---

3   Walvoord, *Revelation of Jesus Christ*, 305.
4   Ibid., 311
5   Ibid.
6   Richard Bauckham, *Word Biblical Commentary*, Vol. 50 (Waco, TX: Word Pub., 1983), 315-321.

importantly, the eschatological coming of the divine Judge."[7] God's judgment should be the focus.

Grudem discusses the debate concerning the new heaven and the new earth. Is it going to be completely destroyed? He summarizes the dialogue between Lutheran scholars and Reformed scholars. According to him, the Lutherans teach an entirely new creation. Reformers emphasize this present creation will be renewed.[8] Grudem identifies with those who teach the earth will be renewed, the Reformed view. He is a proponent of that view.

Concurring with Grudem's renovation view, B. H. Carroll explains his view on Revelation 20:11. "Annihilation is not meant; the flood that swept the earth did not annihilate it; neither does this fire, but it purges it. Peter describes it (2 Pet 3:7, 10, 12)."[9]

McClain shares some interesting insights to this discussion. He interprets Revelation 21:1 as referring to the physical universe.[10] According to him, the first original universe passes away, but then God replaces it with a new universe. He clarifies his understanding of the passage. "This does not necessarily mean the annihilation of our present world of matter, for the Greek *kainos* may mean new in character rather than in substance."[11] He explains the term is used of a regenerated believer when he becomes a new creation (2 Cor. 5:17). The person is not annihilated but transformed.

Vlach concurs with the timing of this new heaven and new earth happening after the millennium.[12] He discusses whether the earth is renovated or annihilated. He sees a discontinuity between the former earth and the latter earth.[13] He concludes the better view is the new earth is renewed rather than annihilated. His reasoning is based on the Bible's storyline (Gen. 1:31), Romans 8, the language of renewal (Matt. 19:28), and the world burned up (2 Pet. 3:10).[14] He says, "The Greek word for 'burned up' is *eurethesetai* and can be translated 'will

---

7   Bauckham, 321.
8   Grudem, 1160-1161.
9   B.H. Carroll, *An Interpretation of the English Bible*, Vol. 6 (Grand Rapids, MI: Baker Book House, 1948), 267.
10   McClain, 510.
11   Ibid.
12   Vlach, 506.
13   Ibid., 509.
14   Ibid., 509-512.

be found' or 'will be laid bare.'"¹⁵ So his view is purification instead of annihilation. He claims that the interpretation supports the purifying meaning.¹⁶

According to Vlach, those who hold the annihilation view base it upon the terminology found in the following:

1. "heavens and earth will pass away with a great noise"
2. "the elements shall melt with fervent heat"
3. "The earth also and the works shall be burned up"
4. "heavens shall be dissolved" (2 Pet. 3:10)

He says, "This restoration is not annihilation but cosmic renewal/regeneration (Matt. 19:28; Acts 3:21) in which God makes all things new."¹⁷ DeYoung argues from the re-creation perspective.

> The first three verses of our devotional passage for today are referring to the time after the Kingdom, as we move into "eternity future" with the "new heavens and the new earth." Notice that the heavens and the earth are not "refurbished," but instead are "created," (Isa. 65:17). This old earth, and the heavens, will be destroyed (2 Peter 3:10), and the Lord will create 'new heavens and a new earth' because the original have been 'cursed' by Satan and his evil angels.¹⁸

This research has revealed that although there are differences of opinion on the exact details concerning the way the new heaven and earth will appear, all agree that this new act of God will take place in the future setting up of His eternal kingdom.

What is meant by "no more sea"? Vlach suggests three options

---

15   Vlach, 512.
16   Ibid., 506.
17   Ibid., 536.
18   Jimmy DeYoung, "Prophetic Prospective Daily Devotional: Isaiah 65:17," Prophecy Today, http://devotional.prophecytoday.com/search/label/Isaiah (accessed December 10, 2018).

for the meaning of "no more sea" (Rev. 21: 1).[19] While water plays an important part in creation (Gen. 1:1-9, 20-22) and the millennium (Ezek. 47), there being "no more sea" is mentioned. He explains the possibilities could be there are no more bodies of water or aquatic life.[20] Second, it could be interpreted figuratively. Some understand it to mean a lack of negative influences on the new earth. Third, it may mean a removal of the salt-water oceans that create a separation between people. Yet, this does not indicate all bodies of water will be absent (Rev. 22:1-2). There will be a "river of the water of life" described in the New Jerusalem. Therefore, there must be some form of water in the New Jerusalem.

What is the biblical description of the New Jerusalem? Where will it reside? How will believers participate in this eternal kingdom? McClain makes an interesting observation. He notes that while mention of the new universe is confined to one verse, there are no less than twenty-five verses in Revelation Chapters 21 and 22 that describe the city in detail. He mentions,

> The record speaks of its 'glory' (v. 11), its 'gates' (vss. 12, 13, 21, 25), its 'wall' (vss. 14, 18), its 'measure' (vss. 15-17), its 'foundations' (vss. 19-20), its 'street' (v. 21), its 'temple' (v. 22), its 'light' (v. 23), its 'nations' (v. 24), its 'river'(v. 22:1), its 'tree' (v. 2), and its 'throne' (v.3).[21]

Revelation 21:2, 9, and 22:5 can also be included. Walvoord points out that the number twelve is prominent. There will be twelve gates, angels, tribes of Israel (Rev. 21:12), foundations (Rev. 21:14), apostles (Rev. 21:14), pearls (Rev. 21:21), and fruit (Rev. 22:2).[22]

What are the dimensions for the New Jerusalem? An angel measures the city. John writes the city is twelve thousand furlongs (Rev. 21:16). Walvoord explains, "Since a furlong is equal to 582 feet, the measured distance is equivalent to 1 342 miles, often spoken of roughly as 1500 miles."[23] Vlach concurs to the size of the city. However, he

---

19 Vlach, 516.
20 Ibid.
21 McClain, 511.
22 Walvoord, *Revelation of Jesus Christ*, 321.
23 Ibid., 323.

mentions several views on the shape of the city. Some hold the city will be cube shape.[24] Others understand it to be in the shape of a pyramid. The third view is the shape of a square. Another debatable feature of this city is its wall. Is it 72 yards thick or high? Regardless, it is massive. Vlach calculates it dimensions based on 1500 miles square. "This means an estimated area of 2, 250, 000 square miles. If correct, the size of this city would reach from Canada to Mexico and from Appalachian Mountains to the California border. This would be roughly half the size of the United States and forty times bigger than England."[25]

Is the new earth and the New Jerusalem the same? Vlach makes several points concerning the differences in the new earth and the New Jerusalem. He says, "If the New Jerusalem is the new earth then the dimensions of this new earth will be dramatically smaller than the present planet.... Also, activity exists outside of the New Jerusalem."[26] He references Revelation 21:24, which reads, "The nations will walk by its light, and the kings of the earth will bring their glory into it." According to Vlach, if the kings are coming in and going out that means activity is taking place on the outside of the New Jerusalem. He concludes, "The New Jerusalem is a city on the new earth and there are geographical locales outside this great city."[27]

Pentecost concurs the two are different. He writes about the church being raptured into the air and then joined by the Old Testament saints when Christ returns to the earth to set up His millennial kingdom. He explains,

> This dwelling place prepared for the bride, in which the Old Testament saints find their place as servants (Rev 22:3), is moved down into the air to remain over the land of Palestine during the millennium, during which time the saints are in their eternal state and the city enjoys its eternal glory.[28]

---

24   Vlach, 519.
25   Randy Alcorn, *Heaven* (Carol Stream, IL: Tyndale House, 2004), 250, quoted in Vlach, 519.
26   Vlach, 518.
27   Ibid.
28   Pentecost, *Things to Come*, 580.

He expounds on the subject by saying, "At the expiration of the millennial age, during the renovation of the earth, the dwelling place is removed during the conflagration, to find its place after the recreation as the connecting link between the new heavens and the new earth."[29] Since the New Jerusalem is distinguished apart from the new earth, it could be the New Jerusalem will be suspended above the new earth.

Walvoord mentions the possibility of a satellite city (New Jerusalem) over the earth during the millennium.[30] "And the nations of them which are saved shall walk in the light of it: and the kings of the earth do bring their glory and honour into it" (Rev. 21:24). He explains, "The word nations (Greek-*ethne*) is the word for Gentiles."[31] These are saved Gentiles who will be in the new city. Therefore, in the church, Jews and saved Gentiles will be in the New Jerusalem.

What is life going to be like in heaven? Pentecost describes a glimpse of life in the eternal city. He says it will consist of fellowship (Rev. 22:4), rest (Rev. 14:13), knowledge (1 Cor. 13:12), joy (Rev. 21:4), holiness (Rev. 21:27), service (Rev. 22:3), satisfaction (Rev. 21:6), and worship (Rev. 19:1).[32] Walvoord adds that God will be present in the new heaven and new earth (Rev. 21:3-4).[33] He comments on the passage, "Behold the tabernacle of God is with men, and he will dwell with them, and they shall be his people and God himself shall be with them, and be their God" (Rev. 21:3). The word "dwell" is the Greek word (*skenoo*) which is translated 'tabernacle' (John 1:14; Rev. 7:15; 12:12; 13:6).[34] The presence of God, according to Walvoord, speaks of fellowship and blessing.

In comparison to the intermediate kingdom (millennium), there will be no more death, neither sorrow, nor crying, neither shall there be any more pain (Rev. 21:4). Walvoord says the words "all tears" is singular in the Greek and literally means "every tear" (Greek-*pan dakruon*).[35] He explains this means every single tear. However, he emphasizes that this does not mean from this text that the saints

---

29   Pentecost, *Things to Come*, 580.
30   Walvoord, *Revelation of Jesus Christ*, 313, 319.
31   Ibid., 327.
32   Pentecost, *Things to Come*, 581-582.
33   Walvoord, *Revelation of Jesus Christ*, 314.
34   Ibid.
35   Ibid., 315.

will shed tears in heaven. Rather, the focus is on the comfort of God not the failure of the saints, and the tears seem to be on earth due to suffering instead of heaven.[36] Since there will not be any more pain, McClain says the following: "Sin is the cause of all tears, all pain, and all death."[37]

Who will be in the New Jerusalem? Will the church and Israel dwell together? Pentecost explains, "The term new Jerusalem is not strictly Jewish in concept, we find Israel has her part in that city, for John (Rev. 21:12) sees the names of the twelve tribes of Israel, indicating that the redeemed of Israel have their part there."[38] However, he clarifies his position. He says, "The city is to be inhabited by God, by the church, by the redeemed of Israel, and by the redeemed of all ages, together with the unfallen angels. However, this city seems to take her chief characteristic from the bride who dwells there."[39]

Jesus leaves the church a message of hope while waiting for His kingdom. McClain writes,

> To the churches on earth, He gives a thrice-repeated reminder of something which must never be forgotten; for it will give courage in the hour of battle, strength in the hour of weakness, and hope in the hour of despair . . .
>
> 'Behold, I come quickly' (v. 7)
> 'Behold, I come quickly' (v. 12)
> 'Behold, I come quickly' (v. 21)[40]

Questions for Review and Discussion

1. What will be the differences during the kingdom period (intermediate) and the time of the New Jerusalem?

---

36 Walvoord, *Revelation of Jesus Christ*, 315.
37 McClain, 514.
38 Pentecost, *Things to Come*, 576.
39 Ibid., 576.
40 McClain, 514.

2. When will the Great White Throne Judgment take place? Cite the scripture references.
3. List the scriptures relating to the Great White Throne Judgment.
4. What will it be like in the New Jerusalem?
5. What last hopeful message did Jesus give to His people awaiting the future (Rev. 22:7, 12, 20)?
6. How does this message give you hope?

Chapter Seven

The King's (Bridegroom) Preparation for His Church Prior to the Kingdom (Rom. 6-8)

What Tony Evans and others are calling "kingdom authority" given to the church, the Scripture describes as Spirit-filled living for believers in the church. That is the power source (1 Cor. 2:4-5; 2 Cor. 4:7). Just because the term "kingdom disciples" is not used to define the church today, it does not mean Christians should have a weak concept of the church. There is resurrection power available for every believer to flesh out the "overcoming life" through the filling and anointing of the Holy Spirit. Yet, there is a major concern to confuse the idea that the church is living presently in the kingdom. Rather than that, as has been proven, the kingdom is futuristic. However, through the power of the Holy Spirit, all believers have been commissioned and enabled to change the world as ambassadors and followers of Jesus until He comes for His church.

Admittedly, Evans is correct in his evaluation of this present culture and the need for the power of God to be experienced through the Holy Spirit. He writes,

> The world today is largely ignoring Christians and

> the church on a myriad of issues because it isn't witnessing the authority we speak about, sing about, pray about, and preach about. What's worse is that many Christians aren't interested in Jesus either. Empty religion has replaced relationship. The church desperately needs people who are on fire from the power of the Holy Spirit, who have a burning desire to proclaim and serve Jesus.[1]

Evans seems to equate this experience, which is available for every believer, with the idea the kingdom of God is now on the earth. Technically speaking, the kingdom will come when Jesus comes to establish it, but not until then. Practically speaking, because of the believer's union with Christ, the inheritance of the kingdom is like heaven. It is the believer's, but not yet. Heaven has not been experienced, but is on its way, and neither have the technicalities of the kingdom. Therefore, clarification, rather than confusion, needs to be given to the body of Christ.

Evans' theological persuasion is the pretribulational and premillennial view. Even he acknowledges the "kingdom" is yet to come. He says, "This glorious kingdom will be ushered in when Jesus Christ returns in what the theologians call His second advent."[2] He may have intensified his views over the years. This was written in 1999, but the earlier quotes are from his latest book written in 2018.

Furthermore, he agrees that Jerusalem will be Jesus' capital.[3] Evans acknowledges Jesus will come back from His throne in heaven to His throne on earth in His millennial reign.[4] Quoting from Revelation 1:7, "Every eye shall see Him, and they also which pierced him," he explains, "This is a reference to the nation of Israel. At Jesus' coming to establish His kingdom, the remnant of Israel that survives the Tribulation will see Him and realize He is their Messiah whom the nation rejected and who was crucified (see Zechariah 12:10)."[5] It appears His eschatology is sound. However, he speculates when he

---

1 Evans, *Kingdom Disciples*, 26.
2 Tony Evans, *Who is This King of Glory?* (Chicago, IL: Moody Press, 1999), 145.
3 Ibid., 147.
4 Ibid., 149.
5 Ibid., 150.

says, "We can model the kingdom right where we are. That's what God wants us to do, set up replicas of Christ's kingdom on earth so people can see what it looks like when Christ controls a person's life."[6] Evans is an articulate and gifted communicator, but he seems to have bought into the progressive dispensational view.

Spirit-Filled Living Versus Kingdom Authority

Has God delegated His power and authority to the church today? Can it be acknowledged without calling it "kingdom authority"? Is God preparing His church to exercise an overcoming life because He overcame (John 10:10; 16:33; 1 John 5:4-5)? Since the kingdom has not come, is the church expected to live defeated lives? Can a Christian rise above the temptations of the world, the flesh, and the devil? Rather than take it to the extreme by calling it dominion authority, there is a balance to avoid the other extreme of defeatism. Through the power of the filling of the Holy Spirit (Eph. 5:18; Gal. 5:16-24; Rom. 8:13; 13:14), the cleansing blood of Jesus (1 John 1:7; Eph. 1:7; Rev. 1:5), the sanctifying work of the cross (Rom. 6:6, 11; Gal. 2:20), and being clothed with the whole armor of God, a believer has all the tools to be an overcomer on a daily basis. This includes positionally, as well as practically. The Christian has been equipped to live a life pleasing to God and to point people to the Savior (John 1:29; 14:6; Acts 4:12).

An exegetical breakdown of Ephesians 5:18, "Be filled with the Spirit," reveals several grammatical truths. The late W.A. Criswell was the pastor of First Baptist Church in Dallas, Texas. He explains the Greek words πληρουσθε εν πνευματι "to be filled with the Spirit" had a special meaning: "To be filled with the Holy Spirit means for us to be so controlled and motivated with the presence and power of the Spirit until our whole being is one perpetual psalm of praise and service to God."[7]

He says that the word is in the imperative mood, which means

---

6 Evans, *Who is This King of Glory?*, 160.
7 W.A. Criswell, *The Holy Spirit in Today's World* (Grand Rapids, MI: Zondervan, 1966), 108.

it is a command. The word is also used in the present tense, which means it is a continuous and ongoing action. Criswell wrote, "The literal translation would be, be ye being continuously filled with the Holy Spirit."[8]

The verb πληρουσθε is in the passive voice. In other words, the subject is being acted upon. The Holy Spirit is acting upon the believer, and finally, the word is plural in number. This means the command is not only to the pastor, but also to the deacon, Sunday school teacher, and all members.

Greek scholar, Joseph Thayer, notes, "Christians are said πληρουσθε, simply as those who are pervaded with the power and gifts of the Holy Spirit."[9]

Walvoord makes an interesting observation. Writing from the dispensational perspective, he explains that all Christians are regenerated, baptized, indwelt, and sealed by the Spirit, but not all Christians are filled with the Spirit. Walvoord clarifies the confusion over the doctrine of the baptism of the Holy Spirit when he writes,

> The Spirit's filling, therefore, is related to experience, which extends over a period of time, in contrast to the baptism of the Spirit, which is often confused. The Greek verb rendered baptized in 1 Corinthians 12:13 is in the aorist tense, which indicates a single definitive act occurring once and for all.[10]

He sums it up best when he states the result of the believer being filled or sanctified is for service unto God.

Through the process of the renewing of the mind, cleansing of the heart, and consequently changing of the will, the Christian experiences a new life in Christ. The message of His glorious appearing should motivate the believer to fulfill his purpose and be ready for the imminent coming of Christ, and then the kingdom. Similarly, the church should be ready to be joined to her bridegroom when He

---

8   Criswell, *The Holy Spirit in Today's World*, 109.

9   Joseph Thayer, *Greek-English Lexicon of the New Testament* (Grand Rapids, MI: Baker Books, 1977), 517.

10   John Walvoord, *Five Views on Sanctification* (Grand Rapids, MI: Zondervan, 1987), 217.

returns, and then to celebrate the marriage supper being clothed in the "righteousness of the saints" (Rev. 19:8). Geoffrey Bromiley defines the word "righteousness"—δικαίωμα—as "righteous deeds of the saints."[11] This righteousness is not to be understood as justification by faith but rather, righteous acts on the part of the saints which comprise the bride of Christ. This will make up the wedding garments of the saints (church) when she is married to her bridegroom.

Fellowship for the Church
Now Preparing for the Kingdom Later

Fellowship with God should be the priority for every follower of Jesus. From the beginning, that was the Lord's intention (Genesis-Revelation). The pages of Scripture reveal how sinful man can walk with His Creator and ultimately glorify God.

The first epistle of John was written to declare that God is light (1 John 1:5-22), love (1 John 4:7-20), and life (1 John 1:1-4; 5:11-13). Therefore, His children will bear resemblance or birthmarks of their Father because of their relationship with His Son, Jesus. Those birthmarks are obedience (1 John 2:3), love for the brethren (1 John 3:14-24), a love for righteousness (1 John 3:6-10), and a discernment of false teachers (1 John 4:1-3).

One of John's purposes for writing this epistle was to refute the Gnostics, those who claimed superior knowledge. Gnosticism had influenced the culture. Some were advocating they had reached a place of sinless perfection. Conversely, others were claiming it did not matter if they sinned. Since they were saved, they had a license to live as they pleased. Both were extremes. Thus, John, inspired by the Holy Spirit, rejected this false teaching. At first there seemed to be somewhat of a contradiction concerning this matter. John clarified when he wrote, "If we say that we have no sin, we deceive ourselves, and the truth is not in us … Whosoever abideth in Him sinneth not: whosoever sinneth hath not seen him, neither known him. Little children, let no man deceive you" (1 John 1:8; 3:6).

---

11   Geoffery Bromiley, *Theological Dictionary of the New Testament* (Grand Rapids, MI: Eerdmans Publishing, 1985), 176.

However, a closer exegetical examination reveals the meaning. John was not promoting the doctrine of sinless perfection. For the believer, God has made provisions to stay in fellowship with Him. First John 1:9 states, "If we confess our sins, he is faithful and just to forgive us *our* sins and to cleanse us from all unrighteousness." However, at the same time he was declaring, because of the believer's changed life, sin was no longer the norm. Therefore, the child of God would not continue in a habitual sinful lifestyle.

> Whosoever sinneth hath neither seen him … he that doeth righteousness is righteous even as He is righteous. He that committeth sin is of the devil, for the devil sinneth from the beginning. For this purpose the Son of God was manifested, that He might destroy the works of the devil. Whosoever is born of God doth not commit sin, for his seed remaineth in him: and he cannot sin, because he has been born of God (1 John 3:6-9).

Doing some grammatical research of the verb tenses will help clarify any confusion. For instance, in verses six and nine the phrase "doth not commit sin" is in the present tense in the Greek. John Stott noted, "Doth not sin is not the isolated act of sin which is envisaged, but the settles habit of it, indicated by the verb *poiein*, to do or to practice."[12]

He further notes that the phrase in verse nine "he cannot sin" (*ou dunantai hamartanein*) is in the present infinitive tense rather than an aorist. If it had been in the aorist it would have meant he was not able to sin, but the present infinitive means he was not able to sin habitually.

The conclusion is inevitable. Since sin continues to be present in those who have been redeemed, purification is God's will for His children in light of His glorious appearing. First John 3:1-3 states,

> Beloved, now are we the sons of God, and it doth not yet appear what we shall be: but we know

---

12   John Stott, *Tyndale New Testament Commentaries, The Epistles of John* (Grand Rapids, MI: Eerdmans, 1989), 126.

that, *when he shall appear*, we shall be like him; for we shall see him as he is. And every man that hath this hope in him *purifieth himself*, even as he is pure.

The challenge is worthy. Since the King is coming to set up His kingdom, the church is presently preparing to join the King. First, the church anticipates the rapture with Jesus as the Bridegroom, and then the second coming of Christ, and finally the church will join the King in His millennial kingdom. This will consummate for the church in the eternal Kingdom in the New Jerusalem.

Questions for Review and Discussion

1. Describe how God prepares the church for the coming kingdom with Holy Spirit filling?
2. Are you a Spirit-filled Christian? If not, why not? Do you need to confess your sins (1 John 1:9)?
3. How can believers be in fellowship with God daily?
4. Are you prepared to share the gospel of Christ (1 Cor. 15:3-4)?
5. Will you trust Jesus as your personal Lord and Savior right now (Rom. 3:23, 6:23, 5:8, 10:9-10, 13)?
6. Are you prepared to give a biblical defense for why you believe "Church Now, Kingdom Later"?
7. Will you pray "Thy kingdom come"?

Conclusion

The goal of this project has been to examine the subject, "Church Now, Kingdom Later." Since the kingdom is the grand theme of Scripture, it deserves an investigation. Starting with the "King's Revelation of the Kingdom" presented in the Old Testament and moving into the New Testament with the "King's Invitation to the Kingdom," the pattern has been set for the study. Often a study of this nature excludes a thorough focus on the church. For that reason, the focus of this study includes, "The King's Evacuation (Bridegroom) of the Church Before the Kingdom" and the "King's Preservation of the Church Before the Kingdom." These elements are absolute when it comes to the proper vision and purpose of the church prior to the kingdom.

President of Southeastern Theological Seminary of the Southern Baptist Convention, Dr. Danny Akin, gives an evaluation of the past eschatological problems when he writes,

> It is very interesting to study the history of Southern Baptists over the last three or four decades because you discover that before 1990 there was a significant disconnect between Southern Baptist seminaries and the people in the pew. At that time, the predominant view of the seminaries was amillennial. There was a small number of pre-millennialists, but they were historical pre-millennial (or post-tribulational,

pre-millennial). The reason for this was the liberalism that had seeped into our seminaries. Now, to be fair, not all amillennialists are theological liberals, but almost all liberals are amillennial. If one denies the full truthfulness of the authority of the Bible and rejects inerrancy and infallibility, it cannot help but impact their hermeneutic.[13]

However, he not only diagnoses the problem but also offers a solution when he explains the following:

Because of this, they do not usually honor the historical grammatical approach to the Scriptures or the literal, plain sense meaning of the text. Or, if they do honor its meaning, they reject its accuracy and truthfulness as to what will actually occur in the future. As a result, they tend to gravitate away from a pre-millennial understanding.[14]

This conclusion by Akin is one of the underlying reasons for this book.

Jesus promises all believers the kingdom will come. Therefore, it seems fitting to study when "The King Inaugurates the Kingdom." Although the fulfillment of this is in the future, assurance for the church is in the present because of the promises kept in the past.

When the final stage of the kingdom concludes on earth, the next phase for the church moves to the "The King's Destination in the Eternal Kingdom."

That leaves the church functioning presently in "The King's Preparation for the Kingdom." Having a biblical understanding of the kingdom in the past and an anticipation for the literal kingdom in the future, gives a believer a clearer purpose and hope in the present.

Jesus not only died for sins and arose from the grave but also promises to come again in the rapture and then the second coming. Immediately following that event, He will set up His kingdom on

---

13   Daniel Akin, http://www.danielakin.com/wp-content/uploads/2009/11/Revised-Manuscript-for-Book-from Acts-1.11-Conference-3.10.10-mg.pdf (accessed December 15, 2018).

14   Ibid.

earth and rule and reign from His throne forever. This is the believer's hope and message for those who are not ready to meet the Lord. He was crucified as the believer's Savior. He conquered the grave as the believer's Lord, and He is coming again as the "KING of KINGS and LORD of LORDS."

Therefore, as Jesus prayed, this truth should motivate every believer with this response, "Thy kingdom come. Thy will be done in earth, as it is in heaven" (Matt. 6:10).

Bibliography

Abbott-Smith, G. *A Manual Greek Lexicon of the New Testament.* Edinburgh: T&T Clark , 1937: 248. Quoted in Joseph C. Dillow. *The Reign of the Servant Kings*. Hayesville, NC: Schoettle Pub., 1992.

Akin, Daniel. "A Rapture You Can't miss, A Judgment You Must Face, A Supper You Will Want to Attend." http://www.danielakin.com/wp-content/uploads/2009/11/Revised-Manuscript-for-Book-from-Acts-1.11-Conference-3.10.10-mg.pdf (accessed December 15, 2018).

Alcorn, Randy. *Heaven.* Carol Stream, IL: Tyndale House, 2004: 250. Quoted in Michael J. Vlach. He Will Reign Forever. Silverton, OR: Lampion Press, 2017.

Allen, Leslie C. *Word Biblical Commentary.* Vol. 29. Dallas, TX: Word Books Pub., 1990.

Allis, Oswald T., *Prophecy and the Church.* Philadelphia, PA: Presbyterian and Reformed Publishing Company, 1945: 69-71. Quoted in Pentecost, *Things to Come.* Grand Rapids, MI: Zondervan, 1958.

Arndt, William F. and F. Wilbur Gingrich. *A Greek-English Lexicon of the New Testament and Other Early Christian Literature.*

Chicago, IL: University of Chicago Press, 1957: 436. Quoted in Joseph C. Dillow. *The Reign of the Servant Kings*. Hayesville, NC: Schoettle Pub., 1992.

_____. *A Greek-English Lexicon of the New Testament and Other Early Christian Literature*. Chicago, IL: University of Chicago Press, 1979: 339, 862. Quoted in Samuel Hoyt. *The Judgment Seat of Christ*. Duluth, MN: Grace Gospel Press, 2011.

Barnhouse, Donald. *Messages to the Seven Churches*. Philadelphia, PA: Eternity Book Service, 1953.

_____. *Revelation: An Expository Commentary*. Grand Rapids, MI: Zondervan, 1971: 43-44. Quoted in Joseph C. Dillow. *The Reign of the Servant Kings*. Hayesville, NC: Schoettle Pub., 1992.

Bauckham, Richard. *Word Biblical Commentary*, Vol. 50. Waco, TX: Word Pub., 1983.

Berkhof, L. *Systematic Theology*. 4th Ed. Grand Rapids, MI: William B. Eerdmans Publishing, 1941: 735. Quoted in Samuel Hoyt. *The Judgment Seat of Christ*. Duluth, MN: Grace Gospel Press, 2011.

Bible Tools. "Adam Clarke Commentary: 1 Corinthians 15:23." Church of the Great God, Inc. https://www.bibletools.org/index.cfm/fuseaction/Bible.show/sVerseID/28742/eVerseID/28742/RTD/Clarke (accessed August 20, 2018).

_____. "Jamieson, Fausset, and Brown Book Notes: 1 Corinthians." Church of the Great God, Inc. https://www.bibletools.org/index.cfm/fuseaction/Bible.show/sVerseID/28743/eVerseID/28743/opt/BN/RTD/JFBBN (accessed August 20, 2018).

_____. "John Wesley's Notes: 1 Corinthians 15:23." Church of the Great God, Inc. https://www.bibletools.org/index.cfm/fuseaction/Bible.show/sVerseID/28742/eVerseID/28742/RTD/jwn (accessed August 20, 2018).

_____. "Matthew Henry Commentary: 1 Corinthians 15:1-33." Church of the Great God, Inc. https://www.bibletools.org/index.cfm/fuseaction/Bible.show/sVerseID/28743/eVerseID/28743/RTD/MH (accessed August 20, 2018).

Blaising, Craig A. and Bock, Darrell L. *Progressive Dispensational*, Grand Rapids, Michigan: Baker Book House Co., 1993.

Blaising, Craig A. and Douglas J. Moo. *Three Views on the Rapture*. Edited by Alan Hultberg and Stanley N. Gundry. Grand Rapids, MI: Zondervan, 2010.

Blomberg, Craig L. *The New American Commentary, Matthew*, Nashville, TN: Broadman Press, 1992.

Blue Letter Bible. "H-4467 – mamlakah – Strong's Hebrew Lexicon (KJV)". https://www.blueletterbible.org//lang/lexicon/lexicon.cfm?Strongs=H4467&t=KJV (accessed October 24, 2018).

Blue Letter Bible. "G-932 – basileia – Strong's Greek Lexicon (KJV)". https://www.blueletterbible.org//lang/lexicon/lexicon.cfm?Strongs=G932&t=KJV(accessed October 24, 2018).

Bromiley, Geoffery. *Theological Dictionary of the New Testament*. Grand Rapids, MI: Eerdmans Publishing, 1985.

Brown, Francis. *The Hebrew and English Lexicon of the Old Testament with an Appendix Containing the Biblical Aramaic*. Edited by S.R. Driver and Charles A Briggs. Oxford: Clarendon Press, 1907: 153-154. Quoted in Samuel Hoyt. *The Judgment Seat of Christ*. Duluth, MN: Grace Gospel Press, 2011.

Bruce. F. F. *The Epistle of Paul to the Romans*. Grand Rapids, MI: Eerdman, 1971.

_____. *Word Biblical Commentary*. Vol. 45. Waco, TX: Word Books Pub., 1982.

Calvin, John. *Commentary on Isaiah.* Vol. 1. Christian Classics Ethereal Library. Grand Rapids, MI: n.d., 66. Quoted in Michael J. Vlach. *He Will Reign Forever.* Silverton, OR: Lampion Press, 2017.

Carroll, B.H. *An Interpretation of the English Bible.* Vol. 6. Grand Rapids, MI: Baker Book House, 1948.

Chafer, Lewis. *Systematic Theology.* Vol. 4-6. Dallas, TX: Dallas Seminary Press, 1948.

Ciampa, Roy E. and Brian S. Rosner. *The First Letter to the Corinthians, The Pillar New Testament Commentary.* Grand Rapids, MI: Eerdmans, 2010: 228. Quoted in Michael J. Vlach. *He Will Reign Forever.* Silverton, OR: Lampion Press, 2017.

Cook, William Robert. "The Judgment Seat of Christ as Related to the Believer." Paper presented to the Professor of Systematic Theology, Dallas Theological Seminary, May 1953: 2-3. Quoted in Samuel Hoyt. *The Judgment Seat of Christ.* Duluth, MN: Grace Gospel Press, 2011.

Cooper, Lamar Sr. *The New American Commentary.* Vol. 17. Nashville, TN: Broadman and Holman, 1994.

Criswell, W.A. *The Holy Spirit in Today's World.* Grand Rapids, MI: Zondervan, 1966.

DeHaan, M. R. *Revelation.* Grand Rapids, MI: Zondervan Pub., 1946.

DeYoung, Jimmy. *Daniel Prophet to the Gentiles.* Chattanooga, TN: Shofar Comm. Inc., 2013.

_____. *Ezekiel: The Man and the Message.* Chattanooga, TN: Shofar Comm. Inc., 2012.

_____. *Jimmy DeYoung's News Update.* http://news.prophecytoday.com (accessed January 16, 2014).

_____. "Prophetic Prospective Daily Devotional: Ezekiel 48:1." Prophecy Today. http://devotional.prophecytoday.com/search?q=Ezekiel+48 (accessed August 20, 2018).

_____. "Prophetic Prospective Daily Devotional: Isaiah 65:17." Prophecy Today. http://devotional.prophecytoday.com/search?q=Ezekiel+48 (accessed August 20, 2018).

_____. "Prophetic Prospective Daily Devotional: Joel 2:28," Prophecy Today. http://devotional.prophecytoday.com/search?q=Joel+2%3A28 (accessed December 23, 2013).

_____. *Ready to Rebuild Revisited: Jewish Plans for the Third Temple*. Prophecy Today, 2011. DVD.

_____. *Revelation: A Chronology*. Chattanooga, TN: Shofar Comm. Inc., 2010.

Dillow, Joseph C. *The Reign of the Servant Kings*. Hayesville, NC: Schoettle Pub., 1992.

Dunn, James. *Word Biblical Commentary*. Vol. 38. Dallas, TX: Word Books, 1988.

Evans, Tony. *Kingdom Disciples*. Nashville, TN: Lifeway, 2018.

_____. *Who is This King of Glory?* Chicago, IL: Moody Press, 1999.

Farnell, David F. "The Kingdom of God in the New Testament." The Master's Seminary Journal 23 (2012): 193-208. Quoted in Michael J. Vlach. *He Will Reign Forever*. Silverton, OR: Lampion Press, 2017.

Feinberg, Charles L. *Millennialism*. Winona Lake, Indiana: BMH Books, 1985.

Feinberg, John S. *Continuity and Discontinuity*. Wheaton, IL: Crossway Books, 1988.

Fruchtenbaum, Arnold G. *The Footsteps of the Messiah*. San Antonio, TX: Ariel Min. 2003.

_____. *Israelology: The Missing Link in Systematic Theology*. Tustin, CA: Ariel Ministries Press, 1989.

Goldingay, John E. *Word Biblical Commentary*. Vol. 30. Dallas, TX: Word Books Pub., 1989.

Got Questions. "What is Christian dominionism?" Got Questions Ministries. https://www.gotquestions.org/Christian-dominionism.html (accessed October 24, 2018).

Gray, James M. "Christ the Executor of All Future Judgments in Christ in Glory." Addresses delivered at the New York Prophetic Conference. Carnegie Hall, November 25-28, 1918. In *Our Hope*. Edited by Arno C. Gaebelein. New York: Publication Office, n.d., 201-202. Quoted in Samuel Hoyt. *The Judgment Seat of Christ*. Duluth, MN: Grace Gospel Press, 2011.

Green, Jay P. *The Interlinear Bible Hebrew-Greek-English*. Peabody, MA: Hendrickson Publishers, 1976.

Grenz, Stanley. *Theology for the Community of God*. Grand Rapids, MI: Broadman and Holman, 1994.

Grimm, Wilibad. *Thayer's Greek-English Lexicon of the New Testament*. Grand Rapids, MI: Zondervan, 1962: 208. Quoted in Samuel Hoyt. *The Judgment Seat of Christ*. Duluth, MN: Grace Gospel Press, 2011.

Grudem, Wayne. *Systematic Theology*. Grand Rapids, MI: Inter-Varsity Press, 1994.

Gundry, Stanley and Darrell Bock, *Three Views on the Millennial and Beyond*. Grand Rapids, MI: Zondervan, 1999.

Hayford, Jack. *Majesty.* Song Lyrics. http://www.songlyrics.com/jack-hayford/majesty/lyrics (accessed November 1, 2018).

Herzig, Steve. *Jewish Culture & Customs.* Bellmawr, NJ: The Friends of Israel, 1997.

Hoyt, Samuel. *The Judgment Seat of Christ.* Duluth, MN: Grace Gospel Press, 2011.

Ironside, H.A. *Revelation.* Neptune, NJ: Loizeaux Brothers, 1981.

Jeffrey, Grant. "Rapture: Three Fascinating Discoveries." Pretribulation Rapture. http://www.pretribulation.com/tag/grant-jeffrey (accessed November 13, 2018).

Keil, Karl and Delitzch, Franz. *Old Testament Commentaries Volume 1.* Associated Publishers, 1861.

Ladd, George Eldon. *The Blessed Hope.* Grand Rapids, MI: Eerdmans Pub., 1956.

_____. *A Commentary on the Revelation of John.* Grand Rapids, MI: Eerdmans, 1972: 260. Quoted in Charles L. Feinberg, *Millennialism.* Winona Lake, IN: BMH Books, 1985.

_____. *A Theology of the New Testament.* 2nd Ed. Grand Rapids, MI: Eerdmans, 1993: 111-119. Quoted in Wayne Grudem, *Systematic Theology.* Grand Rapids, MI: Inter-Varsity Press, 1994.

_____. *Crucial Questions About the Kingdom.* Grand Rapids, MI: Eerdmans, 1952. No page no. Quoted in Gundry, Stanley and Darrell Bock. *Three Views on the Millennial and Beyond.* Grand Rapids, MI: Zondervan, 1999.

LaHaye, Tim, Thomas Ice and Ed Hindson, eds. *The Popular Handbook on the Rapture.* Eugene, OR: Harvest House Publishers, 2011.

Lane, William L. *Word Biblical Commentary*. Vol. 47. Dallas, TX: Word Books Pub., 1991.

Lang, G.H. *Pictures and Parables*. Miami Springs, FL: Conley and Schoettle, 1985: 308. Quoted in Joseph C. Dillow. *Reign of the Servant Kings*. Hayesville, NC: Schoettle Pub., 1992.

Leupold, H.C. *Exposition of Genesis*. Baker Book House, 1942.

Lincoln, Andrew. *Word Biblical Commentary*. Vol. 42. Dallas, TX: Word Books Pub., 1990.

Llewellyn, Chris, Gareth Gilkeson and Will Herron. *Build Your Kingdom Here*. Performed by Rend Collective. Lyrics. https://www.lyrics.com/lyric/28958242/Build+Your+Kingdom+Here (accessed November 1, 2018).

Marshall, I. Howard. *Kept by the Power of God*. Minneapolis, MN: Bethany House, 1969.

Martin, D. Michael. *New American Commentary*. Vol. 33. Broadman & Holman, 1995.

McClain, Alva J. *The Greatness of the Kingdom*. Winona Lake, Indiana: BMH Pub. 1959.

McGee, Vernon J. *Thru the Bible*. Vol 3. Nashville, TN: Thomas Nelson, 1982.

_____. *Thru the Bible*. Vol 4. Nashville, TN: Thomas Nelson, 1983.

_____. *Thru the Bible*. Vol. 5. Nashville, TN: Thomas Nelson, 1983.

Melick, Richard R. Jr. *The New American Commentary*. Nashville, TN: Broadman, 1991.

Merriam-Webster. "kingdom." *Merriam-Webster.com*. 2011. https://www.merriam-webster.com/dictionary/kingdom (accessed October 24, 2018).

Michaels, J. Ramsey. 1960. Review of *The Gospel of the Kingdom* by George Eldon Ladd. *Westminster Theological Journal* 23 (November): 48.

_____. *Word Biblical Commentary 49: 1 Peter.* Dallas, TX: Word Book, 1988.

Miller, Stephen. *The New American Commentary.* Vol. 18. Nashville, TN: Broadman & Holman, 1994.

Moo, Douglas. *The New International Commentary on the New Testament: The Epistles to the Romans.* Grand Rapids, MI: Eerdmans, 1996: 857. Quoted in Michael J. Vlach. *He Will Reign Forever.* Silverton, OR: Lampion Press, 2017.

Moore, Russell D. *The Kingdom of Christ: The New Evangelical Perspective.* Wheaton, IL: Crossway, 2004: 64. Quoted in Michael J. Vlach. *He Will Reign Forever.* Silverton, OR: Lampion Press, 2017.

Moule, H. C. G. *Colossians and Philemon.* Fort Washington, PA: Christian Pub., 1932.

_____. *Philippian Studies.* Fort Washington, PA: Christian Pub., 1927.

_____. *Studies in Ephesians.* Grand Rapids, MI: Kregel Pub., 1977.
Mounce, William D. *The Analytical Lexicon to the Greek New Testament.* Grand Rapids, MI: Zondervan, 1993.

Mounce, Robert. *The Book of Revelation.* New International Commentary on the New Testament. Grand Rapids, MI: Eerdmans, 1977: 352. Quoted in Michael J. Vlach. *He Will Reign Forever.* Silverton, OR: Lampion Press, 2017.

Murray, John. *The Epistle to the Romans.* Grand Rapids, MI: Eerdmans, 1997.

Newell, William. *The Book of Revelation*. Chicago, IL: Grace Publications Inc., 1939.

O'Brien, Peter. *Word Biblical Commentary*. Vol. 44. Waco, TX: Word Books Pub., 1982.

Pentecost, Dwight J. *Designed to be Like Him*. Grand Rapids, MI: Kregal Pub., 1966.

_____. *Prophecy for Today: An Exposition of Major Themes on Prophecy*. Grand Rapids, MI: Zondervan Publishing House, 1961: 154-155. Quoted in Samuel Hoyt. *The Judgment Seat of Christ*. Duluth, MN: Grace Gospel Press, 2011.

_____. *Things to Come*. Grand Rapids, MI: Zondervan, 1958.

_____. *Words and Works of Jesus Christ*. Grand Rapids, MI: Zondervan, 1981.

Polhill, John. *The New American Commentary*. Vol. 26. Nashville, TN: Broadman Press, 1982.

Robertson, Archibald T. *Word Pictures in the New Testament*. Vol. 4. Grand Rapids, MI: Baker Books, 1931.

Robertson, Archibald T. and Alfred A. Plummer. *A Critical and Exegetical Commentary on the First Epistle of Paul to the Corinthians*. 2nd Ed. *The International Critical Commentary*. Edinburgh: T&T Clark, 1941: 65. Quoted in Samuel Hoyt. *The Judgment Seat of Christ*. Duluth, MN: Grace Gospel Press, 2011.

_____. *Critical and Exegetical Commentary on the First Epistle of St. Paul to the Corinthians*. 2nd Ed. The International Critical Commentary. Edinburgh: T&T Clark, 1914: 118. Quoted in Joseph C. Dillow. *The Reign of the Servant Kings*. Hayesville, NC: Schoettle Pub., 1992.

Ryrie, Charles. *Basic Theology*. U.S.A: Victor Books, 1988.

_____. *Dispensationalism*. Chicago, IL: Moody Pub., 2007.

Sargent, Linda. "The Kingdom of God What is It?" Entry posted March 6, 2015. End Time Ministries. https://www.endtime.com/tag/1-corinthians (accessed September 5, 2018).

Schmitt, John and Jimmy DeYoung, dir. *Mysteries of the Temple*. Prophecy Today. DVD.

Schmitt, John and Carl Laney. *Messiah's Coming Temple*. Grand Rapids, MI: Kregal Publishing, 2004.

Schreiner, Thomas R. *The New American Commentary: 1, 2 Peter, Jude*. Nashville, TN: Broadman Pub., 2003.

Showers, Renald E. *There Really is a Difference*. Bellmawr, NJ: The Friends of Israel Ministry Inc., 1990.

_____. *Those Invisible Spirits Called Angels*. Friends of Israel Ministry, Inc., 1997.

Smalley, Stephen. *Word Biblical Commentary*. Vol. 51. Waco, TX: Word Pub., 1984.

Smith, G. Abbott. *A Manual Greek Lexicon of the New Testament*. 3rd Ed. Edinburgh: T&T Clark, 1937: 80. Quoted in Samuel Hoyt. *The Judgment Seat of Christ*. Duluth, MN: Grace Gospel Press, 2011.

Storms, Sam. *Kingdom Come*: *The Amillennial Alternative*. Rossire, Scotland: Mentor, 2013: 301. Quoted in Michael J. Vlach. *He Will Reign Forever*. Silverton OR: Lampion Press, 2017.

Stott, John. *Tyndale New Testament Commentaries: The Epistles of John*. Grand Rapids, MI: Eerdmans, 1989.

Strauss, Lehman. *We Live Forever: A Study of Life After Death.* New York, NY: Loizeaux Brothers, 1947: 73. Quoted in Samuel Hoyt. *The Judgment Seat of Christ.* Duluth, MN: Grace Gospel Press, 2011.

Strong, James. *Strong's Exhaustive Concordance of the Bible.* Nashville, TN: Holman Pub., 1890, 1981.

Thayer, Joseph H. *A Greek-English Lexicon of the New Testament.* Grand Rapids, MI: Baker Book House, 1977.

The Holy Bible-King James Version. Cambridge, UK: Cambridge University Press, 2001.

Thomas, Robert L. *The New American Standard Exhaustive Concordance of the Bible: Including Hebrew-Aramaic and Greek Dictionaries.* Logos Research, 1994.

Toussaint, Stanley D. *Behold the King.* Grand Rapids, MI: Kregel, Inc., 1980.

Trenix, Richard Chenevix. *Synonyms of the New Testament.* Marshallton, DE: National Foundation for Christian Education, n.d., 296-297. Quoted in Samuel Hoyt. *The Judgment Seat of Christ.* Duluth, MN: Grace Gospel Press, 2011.

Unger, Merill F. "The Doctrine of the Believer's Judgment." In *Our Hope.* January 1952: 433. Quoted in Samuel Hoyt. *The Judgment Seat of Christ.* Duluth, MN: Grace Gospel Press, 2011.

Vincent, Marvin R. *Word Studies in the New Testament.* Vol. 1 and 2. Grand Rapids, MI: Eerdmans Pub., 1985.

_____. *Word Studies in the New Testament.* Vol. 3 and 4. Grand Rapids, MI: Eerdmans Pub., 1989.

Vines, W. E. *Vines Expository Dictionary of Biblical Words.* Nashville, TN: Thomas Nelson, 1985.

Vines, W.E. *Vines Expository Dictionary of New Testament Words with their Precise Meanings for English Readers.* Westwood, NJ: Fleming H. Revel Company, 1940: 9, 46, 121. Quoted in Samuel Hoyt. *The Judgment Seat of Christ.* Duluth, MN: Grace Gospel Press, 2011.

Vlach, Michael J. *He Will Reign Forever.* Silverton, OR: Lampion Press, 2017.

Walvoord, John. *Daniel.* Chicago, IL: Moody Press, 1971.

_____. *Every Prophecy of the Bible.* Colorado Springs, CO.: David C. Cook, 2011.

_____. *Five Views on Sanctification.* Grand Rapids, MI: Zondervan, 1987.

_____. *Israel in Prophecy.* Grand Rapids, MI: Zondervan, 1962.

_____. *The Bible Knowledge Commentary.* Colorado Springs, CO.: David C. Cook, 1983.

_____. *The Holy Spirit.* Grand Rapids, MI: Zondervan, 1958.

_____. *The Millennial Kingdom.* Grand Rapids, MI: Dunham Publishing Company, 1959: 59. Quoted in Samuel Hoyt. *The Judgment Seat of Christ.* Duluth, MN: Grace Gospel Press, 2011.

_____. *The Revelation of Jesus Christ.* Chicago, IL: Moody Press, 1966.

Watts, John D. *Word Biblical Commentary.* Vol. 25. Waco, TX: Word Books, 1987.

Waymeyer, Matthew. "What about Revelation 20?" In *Christ's Prophetic Plans: A Futuristic Premillennial Primer.* Edited by John MacArthur and Richard Mayhue. Chicago, IL: Moody Press, 2012: 136.

Wilkinson, Paul and Thomas Ice. "Response to Left Behind or Led Astray." Pre-Trib Research Center. https://www.youtube.com/watch?v=HLWMOdLlSiI (accessed November 13, 2018).

Williams, Gene. *From Now to Eternity*. Conyers, GA: Williams Evangelistic Association, 2004.

_____. *In the Twinkling of an Eye*. Not Available.

Woodring, Chester. "The Millennial Glory of Christ." Master's thesis, Dallas Theological Seminary (1944): 67, 113, 116. Quoted in Dwight J. Pentecost. *Things to Come*. Grand Rapids, MI: Zondervan, 1958.

Yarbrough, Robert W. *The Kingdom of God: Matthew and Revelation*. Edited by Christopher Morgan and Robert A. Peterson. Wheaton, IL: Crossway, 2012: 266. Quoted in Michael J. Vlach. *He Will Reign Forever*. Silverton, OR: Lampion Press, 2017.

Zeller, George. "Weeping and Gnashing of Teeth: Will this be the Fate of True Christians." The Middletown Bible Church. www.middletownbiblechurch.org/doctrine/hodgesgn.htm (accessed September 5, 2018).

Zuck, Roy. The *Bible Knowledge Commentary: New Testament*. Colorado, Springs, CO: David C. Cook, 1983.

About the Author

Randal Dearman Reese

Randy resides in Newborn, Georgia, with his wife Deanna.
They have two grown children, a son Jeremy,
and a daughter Beth Palmer, who is married to Paul.
They have two granddaughters, Larsen and Karmin.

Contact:
pastorrandyreese@gmail.com

Education:
B.A. Luther Rice College and Seminary
M.A. Luther Rice College and Seminary
M.Div. Luther Rice College and Seminary
D.Min. Luther Rice College and Seminary, May 2009
Master of Advanced Prophetics,
Louisiana Baptist University, May 2014
Doctor of Philosophy (Ph.D.) of Advanced Prophetics,
Louisiana Baptist University, May 2019

Pastor
New Rocky Creek Baptist Church
Mansfield, GA, 1991 to present

Bible Prophecy Study, Ph.D.
Trip to Israel, Jordan, Turkey, and Rome 2014

Until That Day Radio Ministry
WJGA Jackson, Georgia, 2017
WDYN Chattanooga, Tennessee, 2017

Books
Tomorrow's Revelation Calls for Today's Purification, 2016
Church Now Kingdom Later, 2019